THE MORTAL INSTRUMENTS COMPANION

ALSO BY LOIS H. GRESH

Nightfall

Eldritch Evolutions

Dark Fusions

The Hunger Games Companion

Blood and Ice

The Twilight Companion: The Unauthorized Guide to the Series

The Fan's Guide to Artemis Fowl

The Fan's Guide to The Spiderwick Chronicles: Unauthorized Fun with Fairies, Ogres, Brownies, Boggarts, and More!

Exploring Philip Pullman's His Dark Materials: An Unauthorized Adventure Through The Golden Compass, The Subtle Knife, and The Amber Spyglass

The Ultimate Unauthorized Eragon Guide: The Hidden Facts Behind the World of Alagaësia

The Truth Behind a Series of Unfortunate Events: Eyeballs, Leeches, Hypnotism, and Orphans—Exploring Lemony Snicket's World

Dragonball Z: An Unauthorized Guide

The Termination Node (with Robert Weinberg)

The Computers of Star Trek (with Robert Weinberg)

Technolife 2020

Chuck Farris and the Tower of Darkness

Chuck Farris and the Cosmic Storm

Chuck Farris and the Labyrinth of Doom

The Science of Superheroes (with Robert Weinberg)

The Science of Supervillains (with Robert Weinberg)

The Science of James Bond (with Robert Weinberg)

The Science of Anime (with Robert Weinberg)

The Science of Stephen King (with Robert Weinberg)

Why Did It Have to Be Snakes? From Science to the Supernatural, the Many Mysteries of Indiana Jones (with Robert Weinberg)

THE MORTAL INSTRUMENTS
COMPANION

CITY OF BONES,
SHADOWHUNTERS, AND THE SIGHT:
THE UNAUTHORIZED GUIDE

Lois H. Gresh

WITHDRAWN

 ST. MARTIN'S GRIFFIN 🍎 NEW YORK

www.stmartins.com

Book design by Richard Oriolo

Library of Congress Cataloging-in-Publication Data

Gresh, Lois H.
    The Mortal Instruments companion : City of Bones, Shadowhunters, and the Sight: the unauthorized guide / Lois H. Gresh. — First edition.
        pages cm
    ISBN 978-1-250-03927-9 (trade paperback)
    ISBN 978-1-250-03928-6 (e-book)
    1. Clare, Cassandra. Mortal instruments.   2. Young adult fiction, American—History and criticism.   I. Title.
    PS3603.L3518Z64 2013
    813'.6—dc23   2013011253

St. Martin's Griffin books may be purchased for educational, business, or promotional use. For information on bulk purchases, please contact Macmillan Corporate and Premium Sales Department at 1-800-221-7945 extension 5442 or write specialmarkets@macmillan.com.

First Edition: June 2013

10 9 8 7 6 5 4 3 2 1

CONTENTS

1 Which Is the Best Book and Movie of All? 1

2 Spinning a Faerie Good Tale 13

3 Romantic Fantasies 33

    What's Up with Romance? 33

    Romantic Triangles 36

    Key Romances 44

        Clary and Jace 44

        Clary and Simon 50

        Clary and Sebastian 53

        Simon and Isabelle 54

        Maia and Jordan Kyle 54

        Magnus Bane and Alec 55

        Jocelyn and Valentine 56

        Jocelyn and Luke 57

        Tessa and William 58

        Tessa and Jem 59

        Nate and Jessamine 61

4 Bad Boys: Who Is the Most Evil? 63

5 Angels and Shadowhunters: The Creation Myth of 67
The Mortal Instruments and The Infernal Devices

6 Mortal Instruments: Cup, Sword, and Mirror 85

7 The Chosen Ones 91

8 Big Bad Mother Demon: Lilith, Her Minions, 97
and Possession

9 Infernal Devices: Automaton Monsters? 111

10 And What About Those Bad Girls? 121

11   Steampunking You   127

12   Resurrecting the Dead and Living Forever   133

13   Alchemy and Ouroboros   153

14   Of Themes and Schemes   159

15   Real or Not Real?   171

Here's How You Play   171
Clary   172
Jace   174
Simon Lewis   175
Isabelle Lightwood   176
Alec Lightwood   176
Raphael Santiago   177
Luke Garroway   177
Valentine   178
Sebastian   178
William Herondale   179
Jem (James Carstairs)   180
Nate   180
Mortmain   181
Mrs. Dark and Mrs. Black   181

16   Opening Conflicts   183

17   Searching for Something   191

Self-Identity Quests   191
Treasure Quests   196
Chasing Mortmain   196

18   Dishing Up the Dirt   197

19   Mini-Biography of Cassandra Clare   203

Notes and Resources   209

WHICH IS THE BEST BOOK AND MOVIE OF ALL?

We're post-Twilight now. Vampires and werewolves are still cool, but fans are clamoring for Cassandra Clare's The Mortal Instruments with all of its angels, demons, warlocks, Shadowhunters, faeries, and of course, vampires and werewolves. Romance, epic fantasy, and good versus evil: What more could you want?

And here comes the *City of Bones* movie, hitting theaters in August 2013. Wow. I wrote companion guides for both the Twilight and the Hunger Games series, and now I'm on the edge of my seat, waiting for *City of Bones*. I've analyzed all three series in detail, immersed myself in the novels—and movies—to the point of obsession. I'm an incredibly huge fan of The Mortal Instruments, probably for all the reasons you're a huge fan.

This book, *The Mortal Instruments Companion—City of Bones, Shadowhunters, and the Sight: The Unauthorized Guide,* gives you a lot to think about, delving into all the reasons we love this series so much. It introduces the many complexities, analyzing key characters and intricate relationships among the more than sixty characters in the first five books of The Mortal Instruments and more than thirty characters in the first two books of prequel The Infernal Devices. These books have everything: multiple plots and subplots, epic romances, intrigue, faerie tales, myths of all kinds wound together, today's world, the steampunk world, and even other dimensions. We have supernatural hunters, relationship struggles, inner conflicts, bad boys, evil mother figures, and of course, angels, demons, faeries, warlocks, vampires, and werewolves: it seems as if *everything's* in The Mortal Instruments and The Infernal Devices.

According to the author, as of August 2012, the first seven books had sold more than ten million copies,[1] and according to the *Wall Street Journal,* had hit twelve million in sales as of June 2012.[2] Fans can't get enough of the action, the supernatural, and the romance. "Discovering a world of supernatural wonder and danger [Clary] joins forces with the Shadow Hunters, a group of warriors whose mission in life is to vanquish the demonic presence in all worlds," writes the *Daily Mail.* "Filled with action, love, magic it's no wonder why the books have become global best-sellers."[3]

It's hard to say which of Cassandra Clare's books I liked the best. Is it *City of Bones,* the first of The Mortal Instruments series, which introduces us to Clary Fray, Jace, Simon, the Shadowhunters, and the Downworlders? Certainly, *City of Bones* sucks us right into the Mortal Instruments universe. This is the book that propels ordinary teen Clary Fray into epic romance and epic fantasy battles as she learns that she's really not ordinary at all.

Is my favorite *City of Ashes,* in which Clary seeks a cure to her mother's magically inflicted coma while battling Valentine and figuring out who and what she is? Is it *City of Glass,* in which Clary goes to Idris and continues to fight Valentine, who now has two of the three Mortal Instruments? Is it *City of Fallen Angels,* in which Jace has nightmares about killing Clary, Simon copes with vampirism, and Sebastian takes over Jace's mind and body? Or is it the fifth book, *City of Lost Souls,* which has me panting for more? I absolutely *cannot* wait for the next book in The Mortal Instruments series.

But of course, I also like both *Clockwork Angel* and *Clockwork Prince* a lot, perhaps because of their steampunk Victorian London settings and cool heroine, Tessa, with her interesting ability to Change. Or maybe I like the (currently) two-book The Infernal Devices prequel because of the clockwork armies and over-the-top characters of Mrs. Dark and Mrs. Black.

It's equally hard to say if I prefer Tessa over Clary, Jace over Will, Isabelle over Jessamine; and where do Jem and Simon fit into my hierarchy of favorite characters? Choices, choices, and more choices.

As of this writing, readers anxiously await the release of *City of Heavenly Fire,* the sixth book—scheduled for 2014—in The Mortal Instruments. Here's what Cassandra Clare says about *City of Heavenly Fire*: "We face in Sebastian an almost unbeatable enemy, and one who knows all of their weak spots. The Shadowhunters are going to lose a lot before they can win this one. So expect a very hard-fought battle and a lot of epic romance."[4] And of course, *Clockwork Princess,* the third book in The Infernal Devices, will be out in March 2013. Because *Clockwork Princess* will be available by the time you have this Companion Guide, I decided not to supply any teasers here. I've read the interviews with Cassandra Clare, so I know it takes place in England and Wales, and that Tessa will have to make some decisions about whom she wants, Will or Jem. This will be a must-read book for all fans of the series. And if that weren't enough, readers also anxiously await The Dark Artifices series, which will take place after The Mortal Instruments ends, with a new generation of Shadowhunters in a very different world.

THE *CITY OF BONES* MOVIE!

While of course Cassandra Clare wrote the *City of Bones* novel, the screenplay is by I. Marlene King and Jessica Postigo. During an interview with *Entertainment Weekly,* Cassandra Clare gave the movie her full support when she commented, "It was very reassuring to come on set and see everything covered in runes and replicated down to the last detail. The movie was definitely made by people who love the books and wanted to do right by them."[5] And as for the rest of us, nobody enthuses about anything in a more vibrant way than Perez Hilton. "We are gnashing our teeth like a demon in heat with SO much excitement for the upcoming screen adaptation of the first book in Cassandra Clare's EPIC science-fiction–fantasy series, The Mortal Instruments."[6]

In this first Mortal Instruments movie, Lily Jane Collins plays the role of Clary Fray. Born in England in 1989, Lily is the daughter of musician Phil Collins and his second wife, Jill Tavelman. The actress has a step–half sister, Joely Collins, who is also an actress, and a half brother, musician Simon Collins, from her father's first marriage to Andrea Bertorelli. Her father had adopted Joely, whose biological father was Andrea Bertorelli's first husband. In addition, when her father remarried again, this time to Orianne Cevey, Lily ended up with two half brothers, Nicholas and Matthew Collins.[7] So she has one younger step–half sibling, one younger half sibling, and two older half siblings—and you thought *your* life was complicated? A half sibling, in case you're one of the lucky few whose parents never divorced and then remarried, means you share one parent, such as a father. In Lily's case, she has a different mother from all her siblings. Okay, now *I'm* starting to feel like Perez Hilton, so let's move on.

When she was two years old, Lily Collins appeared on the BBC program *Growing Pains,* and at five, she moved to Los Angeles with her mother after her parents split up.[8] As a teen, Collins wrote for British magazine *Elle Girl* and also contributed to *Teen Vogue.* She even switched to modeling for a while and appeared in *Glamour* magazine in Spain, where she was the 2008 International Model of the Year.[9] She has since been featured in *Glamour*—for example, in the September 2012 issue when Victoria Beckham decided to feature her. "I was so honored!" Collins remarked about being chosen by Victoria Beckham. "I grew up adoring the Spice Girls. And you can't touch her when it comes to fashion."[10]

Lily Collins returned to the small screen as a model, actually, wearing a Chanel gown on an episode of *The Hills.* She also made a guest star appearance on the reincarnation of *90210,* having attended the same high school (Harvard Westlake in Studio City, California) as original *90210* star Tori Spelling.[11]

She appeared with her boyfriend, actor Taylor Lautner of *Twilight* fame, in the 2011 movie *Abduction,* and then won the starring role as Snow White in *Mirror Mirror,* which was an interesting part for someone destined to play Clary Fray. In *Mirror Mirror,* Snow White duels Prince Charming and even tells him that she doesn't want to hear any more stories about heroines simpering and whimpering and falling apart during times of distress. The actress tells Alison Schwartz and Kristin Luna of

People magazine that "*Snow White* was my favorite fairy tale [growing up], and when I first read about the project, I was like, 'I have to get in on this.' It's such an iconic character."[12]

Speaking of *Twilight* and *Snow White,* Kristen Stewart of *Twilight* fame starred in *Snow White and the Huntsman* after Lily Collins opted out of the role.[13] I can't quite imagine what it would have been like if they'd switched roles, with Lily Collins playing Bella Swan and Kristen Stewart playing Clary Fray. And now that Lily's no longer with *Twilight*'s Taylor Lautner, maybe she'll make room for *City of Bones*'s Jamie Campbell Bower. Do you think?

Cassandra Clare says that the first role to be cast for *City of Bones* was Lily Collins as Clary, and she adds about Collins, "She's extremely dedicated and a really hard worker."[14]

Jamie Campbell Bower, who stars as Jace Wayland in the movie, was born in 1988 to music manager Anne Elizabeth Bower (née Roseberry) and David Bower, who works as an entertainment relations professional at Gibson Guitar and formerly was the director of the Country Music Association in England and Ireland.[15] Before we go any farther, let's pause and think about the fact that Bower is listed as starring in the role of Jace *Wayland.* It's curious that the character has this last name in the *City of Bones* movie, because having read the books, we know that a source of great mystery in the series is the question of who his real father is. For moviegoers who haven't read the books, it would give away too much of the mystery to identify the character as anything else; for example, if Valentine Morgenstern happened to be his father, then Jace *Morgenstern* would be more appropriate. And it would give far too much plot away if the character were identified more accurately as Jace *Herondale.* So, to maintain the mystery and suspense in the movie, it's best to call him Jace *Wayland.*

As with Collins, Bower also comes from an entertainment family, and this helped push him into show business at an early age. He performed as part of England's National Youth Music Theatre (NYMT), also taking the lead singer role in his band. The NYMT boasts a lot of famous alumni (even Jude Law) who have made their marks in entertainment, starring in major feature films and theater productions, including the Royal National Theatre.[16] Bower attended private school in Hampshire and has a younger brother, Samuel.

Is he hunky enough to play Jace? You bet he is. In fact, he looks just like the cover image of Jace on the *City of Bones* book. He stands six feet tall and—another similarity to Lily Collins— has been a model, ranging back to his teen years when he was at Select Model Management. Here's how Melissa Whitworth, who interviewed him in 2009 for the *London Evening Standard,* describes Jace . . . I mean, Jamie Campbell Bower: "The door to the hotel suite swings open and a young man, slightly dishevelled but devilishly handsome, welcomes me in. His jeans are half undone . . . Dressed in cripplingly skinny black jeans with huge rips at the knees ('They are tight, aren't they? Are they throwing you off?'), a thin printed T-shirt and a black hooded top, Jamie could actually, as he says, pass for a prettier Kurt Cobain, with a bit of Russell Brand thrown in. He has wide, feline blue eyes and there's a Gothic-inspired earring dangling from his left lobe."[17]

Formerly engaged to Harry Potter actress Bonnie Wright, their split up reportedly broke his heart.[18] They fell in love during the filming of *Harry Potter and the Deathly Hallows: Part 2,* dated for two years, and lived together in London.

The *Herald Sun* names Bower as a top actor to watch in 2013, noting that "Bower's first leading man test comes with The Mortal Instruments, in which he broods and battles while romancing Lily Collins . . ."[19] Before *City of Bones,* he appeared in a lot of other movies that fans love, including *The Twilight Saga: New Moon* in 2009, *The Twilight Saga: Breaking Dawn,*

Part 1 in 2011, *The Twilight Saga: Breaking Dawn, Part 2* in 2012, *Harry Potter and the Deathly Hollows, Part 1* in 2010, and *Harry Potter and the Deathly Hollows, Part 2* in 2011. In the Twilight films, he played the vampire Caius, a Volturi member, and about *New Moon*, he commented, "I'm a hardcore, die-hard fan."[20] Right before the premier of *Breaking Dawn, Part 2*, he told reporter Jenn Selby that the ending will be "bitter sweet" for Twilight fans. It was November 16, 2012—while I was writing this book—and he was on his way back to the United States to work on *City of Bones*.[21]

With this movie, the casting directors did a pretty good job. Not only did they get Jace right on target, they also nailed Simon Lewis when they cast Robert Sheehan. Like Jace, this actor looks a lot like how I imagined his character while I read the books. Born in Ireland in 1988, Robert Sheehan has appeared in many television programs, films, and theater productions. His parents are Joe and Maria Sheehan, and his older brother, Brendan, is a mortgage broker. Cassandra Clare says on her Tumblr page how pleased she is that Sheehan will play Simon: "He's totally cute and adorable and HILARIOUS, and his chemistry with Lily and Jamie is off the charts."[22] He won the role after hundreds of other actors auditioned for the part.[23]

As for Jemima West as Isabelle Lightwood, Cassandra Clare says, "She had a lot of Izzy's toughness and directness in her audition. I like her."[24] Born in 1987, she grew up in Paris and attended the Sorbonne, where she earned a degree in the history of art. Her father is an accountant, her mother a business interpreter.[25]

Canadian Kevin Zegers, who plays Alec Lightwood, was born in 1984 and has appeared in many movies and shows, including *Gossip Girl, Smallville, Dawn of the Dead*, etc. In late 2012, he told Annette Bourdeau of *Huffington Post TV* that "I'm shooting a film called *The Mortal Instruments,* which is a big fantasy movie. It's . . . running around with swords and fighting vampires and werewolves. I've been having a really awesome time here."[26]

Because he plays a favorite character of mine, I must mention Jonathan Rhys Meyers in the role of Valentine Morgenstern. Born in 1977 in Ireland, Meyers was raised by his mother, who also had three other sons, Jamie, Paul, and Alan. His real name is Jonathan Michael Francis O'Keeffe, but he changed his last name when he started acting, using his mother's maiden name, Meyers. Meyers was actually discovered in a pool hall. From there, he went on to star in a huge number of films, as well as the acclaimed Showtime program *The Tudors.*

You might remember Jared Harris, who plays Hodge Starkweather, from his stint and Emmy for Best Supporting Actor in *Mad Men.* He comes from a showbiz family; his father is the Irish actor Richard Harris, his brother Damian is a director, and his brother Jamie is an actor. Cassandra Clare told Breia Brissey in *Entertainment Weekly* that she was thrilled to have Harris playing Hodge: "He's so great at playing these conflicted characters."[27]

Other actors of note in *City of Bones* are Jonathan Seinen as the Angel Raziel, Godfrey Gao as Magnus Bane, Aidan Turner as Luke Garroway, and Lena Headey as Jocelyn Fray.

It's really no surprise that The Mortal Instruments is shifting to the big screen with the first movie, *City of Bones.* It has a great story and a great lineup of actresses and actors. Most important, it's based on a series of books that experts and fans are raving about.

Because I assume that you've read all the books in both The Mortal Instruments and The Infernal Devices, I'm not including plot summaries here. If you want to refresh your memory about the actual stories, you can read the books again or just look at summaries that you find online. You don't need a companion guide to read the actual novels!

Instead of something simple like a plot summary, this Companion Guide gives you analyses of:

- all the major romances
- angels and Shadowhunters
- the Mortal Instruments themselves
- the chosen ones
- big bad mother Lilith and her demon minions
- steampunk
- the automaton monsters
- resurrection and immortality
- alchemy and the ouroboros
- the major themes in the book
- a huge number of characters
- opening conflicts
- quests in these books
- and more.

In addition, you'll find some discussions about bad boys, bad girls, and humor. And in the back is a mini-biography of the author, Cassandra Clare. I do hope you like this book. I know that I had a lot of fun writing it.

So which is the best book and movie of all? For fans of Harry Potter, Twilight, The Hunger Games, and The Mortal Instruments, it's an extremely tough choice. I can't pick just one, but I do know this: as soon as the next Mortal Instruments book is out, I'm going to get a copy, and the same is true for the next book in The Infernal Devices. Can't wait! You rock, Cassandra Clare!

CONVENTIONS USED IN THIS BOOK

I typically refer to the author's entire name, Cassandra Clare, so readers don't accidentally think I'm referring to the character Clary when I mean Clare.

I typically use the word *faerie* rather than the more standard *fairy* to conform to Cassandra Clare's terminology. I explain why in chapter 2.

VERSIONS OF THE MORTAL INSTRUMENTS AND THE INFERNAL DEVICES REFERENCED IN THIS BOOK

- The Mortal Instruments Series
  - *City of Bones* (book 1). New York: Simon & Schuster, 2007; first paperback edition, February 2008.
  - *City of Ashes* (book 2). New York: Simon & Schuster, 2008; first paperback edition, March 2009.
  - *City of Glass* (book 3). New York: Simon & Schuster, 2009; first paperback edition, August 2010.
  - *City of Fallen Angels* (book 4). New York: Simon & Schuster, 2011; first paperback edition, October 2012.
  - *City of Lost Souls* (book 5). New York: Simon & Schuster, 2012.
- The Infernal Devices Series (prequel to The Mortal Instruments)
  - *Clockwork Angel* (book 1). New York: Simon & Schuster, 2010; first paperback edition, October 2011.
  - *Clockwork Prince* (book 2). New York: Simon & Schuster, 2011; first paperback edition, March 2013.

2

SPINNING A
FAERIE GOOD TALE

There's no doubt about it, at least in this reader's mind: Cassandra Clare spins a faerie good tale—bad pun but so true. She includes updated elements of the classic motifs and tropes of both faerie tales and fantasies. Yet is she spinning faerie tales in the seven current books of The Mortal Instruments and its prequel, The Infernal Devices, or is she spinning paranormal fantasies, dark romantic fantasies, and/or urban fantasies?

Faeries and their myths feature prominently in the novels, and from time to time, characters drop the names of traditional faerie tales. Yet along with the faerie tale references, these books dish up paranormal fantasy characters and epic romances. In addition, they're urban fantasies, as much of the action takes place in New York City (The Mortal Instruments) and London (The Infernal Devices).

This chapter puzzles through just where The Mortal Instruments and The Infernal Devices fit into the scheme of things. Read on and decide for yourself: faerie tale, paranormal fantasy, dark romantic fantasy, and/or urban fantasy? While figuring it out, you'll also discover the underpinnings—that is, the roots of—these novels. Are the ideas entirely new creations, or did the author follow familiar patterns from ancient mythology, traditional faerie tales, and classic fantasy novels?

First, it's obvious that The Mortal Instruments and The Infernal Devices are fantasy series. A fantasy can be set in our real world or in an alternate otherworld.

If set in our real world, such as New York City and London, the story features elements that seem possible in the novel but would be impossible in reality. For example, Clary, Simon, Valentine, Jace, Sebastian, Tessa, Will, and other characters routinely encounter demons, angels, faeries, vampires, warlocks, werewolves, and other supernatural beings in New York City and London. And indeed, the characters themselves are supernatural beings. So while the novels are set in real-world locations, they contain elements that are impossible in reality (as far as modern science knows, that is).

The characters in The Mortal Instruments and The Infernal Devices often use buildings that appear abandoned and vacant to mundanes, ordinary humans like you and me. If not vacant, then part of the structures are invisible or look different to mundanes, or in the case of a cemetery, a Shadowhunter like Will might see ghosts that you and I wouldn't necessarily see. In addition, characters slip into Portals from our real world into other dimensions, which could be thought of as part of the classic fantasy otherworld.

Quite often, critics write about faerie tales and fantasies as if they are the same genre. Folktales and myths sometimes get tossed into the discussion as well. The reason is that the forms of fantasy—its tropes and motifs, its structures and magic systems—overlap between, say, paranormal fantasy and dark fantasy, paranormal fantasy and urban fantasy, and so forth. The boundaries are blurred.

It's interesting to note that The Infernal Devices, which incorporates steampunk and alchemy, also falls on the boundary of fantasy and science fiction. Science fiction is typically lumped with fantasy as being in the same overall genre. You saw in chapter 1 that some people, such as Perez Hilton, refer to The Mortal Instruments as a "science-fiction–fantasy series."

But The Mortal Instruments series tilts far more toward fantasy than science fiction. Fantasy involves magical creatures, objects, and/or events existing in our real world. *Alice in Wonderland* has an Oxford riverbank, *The Wizard of Oz* has a Kansas farm. In fantasy, characters then travel from the real world to magical realms, the otherworlds. At the opening of *City of Bones,* Clary Fray and her friend, Simon Lewis, who live in Brooklyn (specifically, Park Slope), go to the Pandemonium Club in New York City, where they encounter supernatural creatures called Shadowhunters, who are chasing demons. It's here that Clary meets Jace, Isabelle, and Alec for the first time. It is at the Pandemonium Club, set in our real world, that Clary first has the Sight—that is, she sees the Shadowhunters and the shape-changing Eidolon demon, and mere mundanes aren't supposed to be able to do that. The entire demon chase scene, including Clary's unfolding Sight, are magical events that exist in our real world. At the opening of *City of Glass,* Clary intends to travel to Idris in another dimension to save her mother, Jocelyn. Idris represents part of the otherworld, the magical realms, in The Mortal Instruments.

You may have heard of or even read Joseph Campbell's famous book *The Hero with a Thousand Faces*. We often talk about this book on writing panels at science-fiction and fantasy conventions. For example, at I-CON at SUNY Stony Brook a few years ago, I was on an hour-long panel that talked exclusively about parallels between Campbell's *The Hero with a Thousand Faces* and George Lucas's Star Wars. It's common knowledge that Lucas admired Campbell and structured Star Wars based on what Campbell termed the *monomyth,* the notion that in all cultures throughout history, people have told the same story over and over again, just with different heroes.

The Mortal Instruments and The Infernal Devices also fit into the monomyth concept, as you'll see below. This is a large reason why it's so popular. Stories that follow Campbell's hero cycle, fusing magic and mythology—whether it's Star Wars, Lord of the Rings, or The Mortal Instruments—touch us deeply on an emotional level and urge us to find order and meaning in our world. The hero cycle incorporates villains, mentors, adventures, obstacles, morals, ethics, and the search for truth and identity.

Joseph Campbell, who knew Carl Jung, incorporated the psychologist's ideas about archetypes into *The Hero with a Thousand Faces*. In Jung's lingo, an archetype is a standard type of character we see in myths from all times and from all around the world. Jung thought that human beings subconsciously divide our minds into various archetype characters, such as young hero, shape-changing girl, and shadowy enemy. The parallel here is that Jace and Will are young heroes, Clary and Tessa are young heroines, Tessa is a shape-changing girl, and characters such as Valentine, Sebastian, and Mortmain are shadowy enemies.

Mythic heroes grow up without knowing that they have special gifts and powers, that they come from royal or otherwise special families. A series of teachers helps the heroes recognize, use, and tame their special gifts.

In The Mortal Instruments, Clary comes from what we might think of as a royal or an otherwise special set of parents. At first, she doesn't have a clue about her real background because her mother, Jocelyn Fray, has gone to extraordinary lengths to keep it from her. We learn in *City of Bones* that Valentine Morgenstern is her real father, and in a way he's a form of evil royalty such as Darth Vader in Star Wars. Valentine hated the idea of the Accords, as proposed by the Clave to provide peace with the Downworlders, and so he created the Circle of Raziel, Shadowhunters who aimed to kill Downworlders and cleanse the world of them. This makes Valentine a leader, just like Darth Vader, someone at the top of a hierarchy of evil. Jocelyn could be viewed as the wife of this Nazi-like evil prince.

Am I overstating their "royal" status and Valentine's Nazi-like attitude? I don't think so. Valentine tortured everybody to death. Attempting to create superwarriors, he documented his experiments—just like the Nazis—in which he tortured werewolves, vampires, and other creatures. He drank angel blood and even doped up his wife, Jocelyn, with it when she was pregnant with Clary. This bizarre "royal" family of Clary's also included the part-demon boy, Sebastian Verlac. You see, her family is different from all others, special, elevated to a different status, and whether her family status is good or bad, Clary must learn to tame and use her special gift of creating new runes, a gift she possesses because she has angel blood.

Who are the people who help Clary recognize, use, and tame her special gift? Offhand, they include teens such as Jace Wayland and Isabelle Lightwood as well as adults such as Hodge Starkweather, Magnus Bane, and Luke.

And what about Tessa Gray in The Infernal Devices? Like

Clary, she also comes from what we might think of as a royal or otherwise unusual set of parents. We know from the beginning that her mother died wearing a special clockwork angel pendant, which we later learn has special properties. This factor alone makes her mother unusual, special, unique. Whenever Tessa channels dead people and Changes into either the living or dead, the clockwork angel pendant ticks faster. Further, when the evil automatons get near the pendant, sometimes they recoil. Apparently, sometimes the pendant protects her, but at other times it does not. Nobody else's mother—as far as we know—possessed a pendant with this type of power, so Tessa's mother must be elevated to a special status, just like Clary's mother. Both mothers are different from, say, Simon's mother, who is a mundane, or even Isabelle's mother, a powerful Shadowhunter. Tessa's mother is something more powerful; we just feel it before we even know who she is. We learn very little else about her, and when Jessamine says that she was a Shadowhunter, this is never verified for Tessa, so we don't know whether that's true. Tessa's bloodline remains a mystery.

At first, like Clary, Tessa doesn't have a clue about her real background. She doesn't even know *what* she is: human, warlock, or something else. At first, she's confused as to what she is, just like everyone around her is confused about it. Charlotte and Brother Enoch tell her she's a Downworlder—which includes vampires, werewolves, faeries, and warlocks—most likely an Eidolon, a shape-changer, probably a warlock. The problem is that she has doesn't have warlock marks, such as taloned hands, webbed toes, hooves, or wings. Another clue we get is that Brother Enoch senses that she has a power she doesn't yet know. We're constantly told that Mortmain "made" her, though by the end of *Clockwork Prince,* we still don't know what that means. We get another clue when Hyacinth tells Tessa that she will not age or die. The sum total of these clues is *mystery.*

Who are the people who help Tessa recognize, use, and tame *her* special gift? Oddly, her first mentors are the Dark Sisters. She discovers from them—in a most unpleasant way—that she has the ability to Change, and they force her to learn how to use her gift and tame it. Her other mentors include teens such as Will Herondale and James Carstairs, aka Jem, as well as adults such as Charlotte Branwell and good old Magnus Bane (one of my favorite characters).

Stretching back to ancient mythology through Lord of the Rings, Star Wars, and The Mortal Instruments, fantasies use the basic concept of a quest to bring out their heroes' abilities and true characters. You can also think of the main quest in a fantasy as a search for the hero's self-identity, sometimes called the awakening of the self. This is when the hero finds out what she's really made of: brave, smart, strong, willing to sacrifice for others, caring, kind. Every expertly written quest pits the hero against evil out to destroy goodness in the world, propels the hero into challenges in which she could die, and requires that she take action to keep the world good, balanced, and in peace. The hero must become a leader of her people. At the core are the ideas of good versus evil as well as the awakening of self. When asked why people read paranormal romance, editor and publisher Paula Guran explains, "Is it the human desire for the numinous and the need to uncover the transcendent beneath the mundane? That might sound pretentious, but that's the power that underlies any fantasy. Fantasy is a way of seeking significance in life, something beyond the ordinary that our rational, logical, scientific culture doesn't offer. The irrationality of magic and the supernatural attracts us. Plus, strong, intelligent female protagonists satisfy and empower."[1]

The major aspects of Campbell's hero cycle fantasy are outlined below. For demonstration purposes, I'll draw parallels between Campbell's outline and, to simplify matters, focus mainly on *City of Bones* of The Mortal Instruments and *Clockwork Angel* of The Infernal Devices. Keeping in mind that we don't yet have the final novels in these series, it's best to focus on the first novels in each, though I have pushed forward a bit and supplied additional details as necessary. Because both are sagas, you can fill in the outline with details from subsequent books in the series.

- The hero—or heroine—begins in his ordinary world. For Luke Skywalker in Star Wars, it's a farm where he lives. For Clary, it's Brooklyn. In both The Mortal Instruments and The Infernal Devices, shadows are everywhere as a major motif. Possibly the shadows represent darkness while the angels (and Jace) represent light.

- The hero encounters a challenge or problem that requires adventure. Princess Leia in Star Wars sends a holograph message to Obi Wan Kenobi, who requests Luke Skywalker's help on a quest. For Tessa, the Dark Sisters kidnap her and torture her in the Dark House to teach her how to Change into other characters. For Clary, she encounters Shadowhunters and demons at the Pandemonium Club, and soon after discovers that her mother is gone.

- The hero is reluctant to go on the adventure or quest. Fear of the unknown can be powerful, and characters need motivation to risk their lives. Luke Skywalker doesn't instantly agree to Obi Wan Kenobi's request for help. Instead, he returns home to the farm, where he finds that storm troopers have attacked his aunt and uncle. Now he wants to fight the Emperor. Tessa resists the Change and tries to escape from Mrs. Dark and Mrs. Black, and in particular, she fears the Magister, who wants to possess her for unknown reasons. In Clary's case, Jace wants her to come to the Institute to learn about Shadowhunters and Downworlders from Hodge, who specifically requests her presence. At first, she doesn't want to go. But her mother disappears, she must fight a Ravener demon in her home, and Jace tells her she'll die quickly from Ravener poison unless she comes to the Institute. Clary quickly changes her mind.

A wise old man or woman serves as a mentor to the hero. Obi Wan Kenobi gives Luke Skywalker a lightsaber and serves as a wise old being in Star Wars. Obi Wan and Yoda teach Luke to harness the Force for good, and by doing this, Luke develops into a young man with a grand purpose. For a long time, Hodge is the wise old man of The Mortal Instruments. Perhaps Charlotte is the young wise woman of The Infernal Devices. In both series, Magnus Bane offers help and knowledge constantly. He summons demons, he conjures spells. Luke Garroway is also an adult mentor to Clary. But perhaps the mentoring of both Clary and Tessa comes primarily from other teenage characters such as Jace, Will, and Jem. In modern young adult fantasies, it's often the protagonist's friends who serve as her mentors because in today's real world, it's often your friends who provide you with support and advice, encouraging you and helping you navigate through personal obstacles and challenges. As readers of The Mortal Instruments and The Infernal Devices, who do you think serves as Clary's and Tessa's mentors?

The adventure begins. Luke Skywalker sets off to fight the Emperor. William saves Tessa from the Dark Sisters. Jace brings Clary to Hodge at the Institute.

The hero overcomes challenges that block his path to final victory, and along the way he makes allies and enemies. Luke Skywalker battles the Imperial fighters and learns how to use his lightsaber. He also finds an ally in Han Solo and an enemy in Jabba the Hut. Tessa must learn how to control the Change, and she must find her supposed brother, Nate. Tessa and allies

Will, Jem, and Jessamine (among many others) fight automaton after automaton. Enemies include Valentine, Sebastian, and Mortmain, among others. Clary must overcome a block in her mind that seals her memories, and she must find her mother. Clary and allies Jace, Simon, Isabelle, and Alec (among many others) fight demon after demon. An emerging enemy is Raphael the vampire. Another enemy is Valentine (among others). These are just a few examples of challenges, allies, and enemies in the approximately thirty-five hundred pages of the first seven books of The Mortal Instruments and The Infernal Devices.

■ The hero confronts his or her most extreme challenge. She has life-or-death experiences, and in many cases she goes through death and rebirth, emerging as a better person. All readers identify with these struggles. All of us confront these challenges, in which we must make serious choices and emerge as either better people or worse people. Often, an actual life-or-death experience—serious injury, the loss of a friend or family member, an event such as a hurricane or other natural disaster—brings out our true nature. Tessa promises to marry Mortmain if he lets everybody else go, and then she stabs herself in the heart. Toward the end of *City of Bones*—and again, this outline focuses mainly on *City of Bones*—Clary figures out where her mother hid the Mortal Cup.

■ The hero fights hard and wins the final battle with the villain, which Carl Jung called the Shadow archetype. Luke rescues Princess Leia and now will fight the Shadow archetype, Darth Vader. Han Solo saves Luke from Darth Vader. When battling Shadow archetype Mortmain, Tessa almost dies. Right before the knife touches her, she Changes quickly into a dead girl she'd Changed into back when she was imprisoned by the Dark

Sisters. In *City of Bones,* Clary figures out where her mother
hid the Mortal Cup from Valentine.

◼ The hero acquires whatever he or she has been seeking:
treasures, weapons, elixirs, or knowledge. The rebellion beats
the evil Empire. For now, the clockwork army has been
defeated, and Tessa remains at the Institute. Clary finds her
mother.

This is a very streamlined look at the classic structure. In
general, when fantasy novels conform to this structure and are
well written, they tend to work for readers. The reason is that
the heroes, or protagonists, develop as human beings during
their quests. Readers like to empathize with protagonists, they
like to feel their heroes' angst, emotions, pain, and joy. The arc
of the structure allows protagonists to do all of these things.
They struggle and overcome great obstacles and challenges.
They're forced to make moral and ethical decisions. If they do
wrong, all hell breaks loose. If they do right, then the world become a better place. The heroes tend to have high morals and
they put the welfare of other people before their own well-
being. If a hero is an ordinary person in the beginning of the
story, he or she will end up being more introspective, more caring, more giving, and less selfish by the end. She will have found
her inner strength. The journey is far more than the one over
space and time and against evil. It is also an internal journey for
the hero.

As an aside, I wonder if Cassandra Clare uses the name
Luke (as in Luke Galloway) so we subconsciously feel that The
Mortal Instruments is an epic fantasy along the lines of Joseph
Campbell's classic structure, the very one used in Star Wars. She
does use many biblical names in her books, Luke being one of
them, so perhaps his character name blends twin connotations
of biblical power with Star Wars power.

Young adult fantasy series such as The Mortal Instruments and The Infernal Devices are particularly adept at connecting readers to protagonists. Most key heroes are young and coming of age. Most are teenagers, as are Clary, Jace, Simon, Alec, Isabelle, Tessa, Will, Jem, and Jessamine. Most teens are trying to find themselves. No longer children, they aren't quite adults, either. They don't yet know what they'll do during their lifetimes, which occupations they'll find interesting, whom they'll marry, whether they'll have children, where they'll live, how they'll change as they emerge from the cocoon of teenage years into full-blown adult independence. This is probably why, when we're teenagers, we question everything and everyone. There are so many forks in the road at this stage. And in addition, when we're teenagers, we grapple with everyday problems, such as just how to be true to ourselves, stick to our guns, so to speak, without becoming social pariahs. Nobody wants to be an outcast. Yet we don't want to sacrifice how we really feel and who we really are, either.

The heroes of young adult fantasy novels face all of these questions. They faced these questions in Philip Pullman's His Dark Materials trilogy, in J. K. Rowling's Harry Potter novels, and also in Suzanne Collins's The Hunger Games. And in each of these series, the heroes act based on their consciences; they don't fall prey to evil in their worlds, and hence, they're able to perform their heroic acts. The same is true for Clary, Jace, Simon, Tessa, Will, and Jem. The reason you love them is that you identify with them on some level, you understand what they're going through even though they're doing it all in fantasy worlds.

Fantasy novels enable you to view familiar situations, such as those just described, within the context of an imaginary world. The fantasy worlds step outside our everyday existence yet touch us at the core about human emotions and conflicts, including notions of good versus evil and right versus wrong.

Reading fantasy helps us view our problems and arrive at solutions with fresh perspectives. It's all under the hood. We're not conscious of this happening. We just think we're reading a great story. But part of the reason we love the story so much is that we identify with the problems of the heroines and heroes, and by seeing how they cope with the problems, maybe it helps us feel a little better about dealing with our own problems.

In addition, when you consider the complexity of the fantasy world, you see that sometimes in the midst of all the obstacles, challenges, problems, and confusion, we as readers just want to be reminded—like a hug from a good friend—that basic goodness and truth will prevail, that holding our heads high and ignoring mean-spirited people, or what we view as actual evil, is okay. It's reassuring to be reminded about the basic wisdom—about good versus evil, about kindness versus nastiness, about strength versus weakness, about making sacrifices for others versus being selfish—that we wish everybody could possess.

What's truly interesting is Cassandra Clare's very public stance about bullying and Internet stalkers who have harassed her, as well as her readers and other authors: "I get a huge amount of e-mail from young girls and women, who make up the bulk of my readership, who are the target of a very specific kind of online cyberbullying . . . you *are* great because you make fanart/gifs/cosplay/write book reviews/post pictures of yourselves looking pretty. Because it's hard to put yourself out there, to put any creative work or any part of your personality out where it can be judged (and it will be!). Because it's hard to tell people how you really feel."[2]

It takes guts to stand up and take a position on this issue. Most of us—certainly, most authors with a large readership—have been harassed by Internet stalkers and bullies. It drives us to write more fiction because we feel compelled to explore the basic *wrongness* of this type of personality. The Mortal Instruments is about good versus evil, about kindness versus nastiness, about strength versus weakness, about making sacrifices for others without being selfish. These books clearly display the heart and soul of their author.

Clearly, The Mortal Instruments and The Infernal Devices are within the realm of dark paranormal fantasy, as are J. K. Rowling's Harry Potter books. Paranormals are booming with teens as well as adults, and novels have everything from vampires and werewolves to angels and demons to ghosts, wizards, witches, dragons, and every other type of supernatural creature imaginable. Other examples of dark paranormal fantasies for teens are P. C. Cast's House of Night series, Julie Kagawa's The Iron Fey and Blood of Eden series, Cynthia Leitich Smith's *Tantalize, Eternal, Blessed,* and *Diabolical,* Lynn Viehl's Youngbloods, as well as many more. There are endless choices for teenagers interested in reading about werewolves, vampires, demons, angels, faeries, shape-shifters, wizards, trolls, zombies, ghosts, and much more.

The Mortal Instruments and The Infernal Devices also are romantic fantasies, which incorporate many of the conventions found in romance novels. The basic idea is that two people fall in love, their love is constantly tested, and in the end, love wins and they live happily ever after. While regular—that is, nonparanormal—romance novels enable readers to explore their fantasies with the glow of a happy ending, paranormal romances also enable readers to think about how magic might enhance the romantic experience. Supernatural creatures have special gifts and heightened senses, which make their romances much more diverse and powerful. Included in this romance subgenre are gods, vampires, werewolves, wizards, angels, faeries, and any other exotic beings that authors can concoct.

But The Mortal Instruments and The Infernal Devices also

qualify as urban fantasy because they take place largely in New York City and London. "When I was growing up in the '80s," the author tells journalist Stephen Jewell, "there was a sort of cult movement of writers who were popularizing this idea that you should bring fantasy into the modern world. For me, that was much more relatable than traditional high fantasy, which was all very medieval with castles and knights. I couldn't connect with that as a twelve-year-old girl but I could connect with the idea of children or teenagers running away from the real modern world to join a semi-magical world."[3] In addition, she tells Andrea Ong in the *Straits Times,* "I've always found there to be something magical about Manhattan, despite—or may because of—its dense urban landscape."[4] Urban fantasy is today's magic realism, and its fantasy elements blend into modern environments.

In addition, The Mortal Instruments and The Infernal Devices qualify as faerie tales—hence the title of this chapter, "Spinning a Faerie Good Tale." Of course, The Infernal Devices fits into the steampunk genre, as well, but I talk about that in chapter 11.

I should point out that Cassandra Clare uses the word *faerie* rather than the standard *fairy* that we see in the common term *fairy tales.* The English word *fairy* is derived from the Old French word *faerie,* which means "enchantment." Traditionally, the land of the fairies is known as Faerie or Fairyland. Faerie is actually an otherworld linked to our real world. In *City of Ashes,* Jace, Simon, and Clary need to gain access to Faerie, which is underground, and they go through a forest and a lake to get there. The forest and the water are standard methods of reaching Faerie, and originally, Faerie as an otherworld was actually an *underworld,* where people went after they died, so perhaps this is why it's often found underground. Traditionally, Faerie is timeless, meaning fairies can be there for centuries within a mere split second of our Earth time. In *City of Ashes,* we're told that "faeries live for hundreds of years." This implies that they do die at some point. However, we're also told that faeries "are the offspring of demons and angels," which implies immortality, and in *City of Glass,* Valentine says that faeries are immortal.

By the way, to simplify matters, throughout *The Mortal Instruments Companion,* I'll use Cassandra Clare's term *faeries* for the actual creatures rather than their homeland.

Her novels incorporate many types of faeries, all of them Downworlders. Remember, Downworlders are part supernatural in origin and include faeries, vampires, werewolves, warlocks, and also zombies, which don't appear in the first seven novels. Apparently, angels and demons are not included.

Among the many references to specific faerie tales in The Mortal Instruments and The Infernal Devices are *Alice in Wonderland* (*City of Bones,* pages 109 and 462); *Cinderella* (*City of Bones,* page 171); *Snow White* (*City of Fallen Angels,* pages 323–324, and *City of Glass,* page 445); and *The Little Mermaid* (*City of Lost Souls,* pages 157–158).

Faerie tales are forms of fantasy with supernatural characters and elements. Just like fantasies, faerie tales mediate between the way we really live and the way we might prefer to live. Characters possess magical powers and amazing wisdom, and heroes may have to overcome obstacles using supernatural mechanisms and the help of allies. Villains may threaten to kill the heroes and their loved ones, and other characters may request that the heroes perform demanding tasks. Typically, the main characters are young and, as the faerie tale opens, not treated particularly well. Faerie tales, like the Joseph Campbell fantasies, are about growing up and finding oneself, about becoming self-sufficient and independent, about discovering what matters in life. When heroes are strong, kind, and intelligent, when they behave in moral and ethical ways, when they help others even at risk to themselves, they develop into mature leaders who find their soul mates.

Traditional faerie tales are short, and many go back thousands of years, stretching into the oral folklore of people around the world. They move quickly and provide very little background about characters. While faerie tales are a form of fantasy, clearly not all fantasies are faerie tales.

In many classic faerie tales, heroes first leave their homes and are either orphans or must leave their parents. Often, they have purposes in life that they don't yet know about, and after they set off on their quests and adventures, they wind up having new homes and families. All of these factors are true for The Mortal Instruments and The Infernal Devices. After Jocelyn disappears, Clary winds up becoming part of the Institute family. After Will saves Tessa from the Dark Sisters, she too winds up becoming part of the Institute family. Simon's mother barricades the front door of the house to keep him out. Jem, Isabelle, Jace, Jessamine, and Alec are all on their own. All the Shadowhunter teens live at the Institute as an adopted, new form of family with adult leaders such as Hodge Starkweather, Charlotte Branwell, and Maryse Lightwood.

In many classic faerie tales, young girls find their princes and shift from childhood to finding love, kissing (and more) for the first time. They experience emotional turmoil just like real teenagers do. The love fluctuates from intense to cool, intense to cool, with the girl wondering whether he loves her and, if so, what this even means.

When the Iron Sisters make demon towers and Shadowhunter steles, witchlights, seraph blades, and runes out of adamas, it's almost as if they're making magical objects out of an earthly substance. This reminds me of spinning gold out of straw, another magical method of transforming an earthly substance into something of great value. Or when Clary shapes totally new runes in her mind that become real, isn't she also creating gold out of straw? Perhaps these ideas about females creating things where nothing existed before stretch back to the dawn of time, when people worshipped Mother Earth and motherhood. After all, one of the recurring themes in faerie tales is the female cycle of fertility, of giving birth to the world: youth to fertile teen to mother to elderly woman—typically called the "crone," which certainly has a negative connotation.

Speaking of crones at the far end of the female cycle of fertility, consider Lilith, the mother of all demons, who was Adam's first wife—before Eve. The first of all demons, Lilith refused to obey both God and Adam, and she left the Garden of Eden, so God cursed all of her children to death upon their births. Cassandra Clare cleverly solves the problem of how Lilith gave birth to all the demons by telling us that Lilith scattered her blood and the drops became the demons.

In some ways, Lilith reminds me of Snow White's stepmother, who despises Snow White for being young, beautiful, and still able to find love and have children. In fact, the stepmother despises her own daughters, too, because of their youth. Lilith is so angry and jealous of young women that she kills human infants. You might say she's the demon goddess of dead children.

When Tessa chooses Jem over Will because she can't bear to hurt Jem, the reader wonders if she's really going to go through with it and marry the wrong guy. This reminds me of Sleeping Beauty, who marries the wrong guy when she wakes up from her long sleep. And consider Clary. She knows in her heart that Jace is the only guy for her, and yet she fluctuates constantly—albeit with good reason—and almost ends up with the wrong guy, Simon and briefly, we fear, even Sebastian. For Clary, who is her real prince, Jace or Simon? For Tessa, who is her real prince, Will or Jem? What do you think? I believe that Jace is clearly Clary's soul mate and Will is clearly the one for Tessa.

But Cassandra Clare sets things up in a classical sense and leaves us spellbound, worrying that our heroines will make the wrong choice. The author knows how to spin a faerie good tale, indeed (and don't worry, that's the last time I'll use that pun).

Let's stretch our imaginations to Hansel and Gretel for a moment. Gretel shoves the witch into the oven and saves Hansel. The girl saves the boy. Well, Clary saves Jace when she uses the sword of the Archangel Michael to sever the connection between Sebastian and him. Go back and read pages 493–496 in *City of Lost Souls*—the description of Jace's transformation into a golden angelic creature is beautifully done, isn't it? But back to Gretel being the one who saves Hansel, and Clary being the one who saves Jace: it takes a lot of courage and intelligence for Clary to figure out how to save him. Remember, she stabs him with a sword! *City of Bones* even mentions Hansel and Gretel briefly on page 161, when Clary is dreaming about Simon and Jace. At the end of the dream, she sees Isabelle and Alec, "holding hands like Hansel and Gretel in the dark forest."

And now, swing back to "Rumpelstiltskin" and all that straw being spun into gold. Remember, the miller's daughter is locked in a room in a tower, and the only way out is to create something in a way that's never happened before, almost out of thin air. Symbolically, the Portals may be like the locked door in "Rumpelstiltskin." To overcome obstacles and solve problems, characters must find ways through these locked doors, or Portals. Clearly, internal doors abound, as when Clary creates the new runes.

Finally, a note about Walt Disney's versions of faerie tales and how this jibes with The Mortal Instruments and The Infernal Devices. Walt Disney created films in which the girls are passive and hoping for romance as their princes battle evil creatures who are trying to possess them. The girls typically ended up with romance novel endings, living happily ever after with their Prince Charmings. While both The Mortal Instruments and The Infernal Devices feature strong heroines rather than passive ones, they include heroes and romance as well as evil creatures who fight to possess the girls. For example, Mortmain as the Magister wants to marry Tessa and control her unusual shape-shifting abilities. In "Rumpelstiltskin," the king wants to possess the miller's daughter and control her unusual ability to spin straw into gold. Sebastian Verlac needs Clary to drink from the Infernal Cup so he can raise Lilith and proceed with his evil plan to create a new demon population. Jace is under his spell, Amatis is under his spell, and now he needs Clary under his spell, as well.

So how would you classify The Mortal Instruments and The Infernal Devices? Are they paranormal romantic fantasies, are they urban fantasies, are they faerie tales, or as I believe, do they have elements of all?

Thus far, I've touched only briefly on the vast number of topics in The Mortal Instruments and The Infernal Devices. There is *so* much in these books to talk about, *so* much depth, and yet these books are so much fun to read that you can't put them down. You can read the entire series multiple times and still discover new things. These are the marks of a faerie . . . I mean, a *very* good tale.

3

ROMANTIC FANTASIES

WHAT'S UP WITH ROMANCE?

This chapter explores the epic romances of The Mortal Instruments and The Infernal Devices. Why is romance so popular these days? What are the fundamental rules of writing romance, and how well does Cassandra Clare pull it off? Who are the lovers, what keeps them apart, how do they overcome their problems (or not), and how do they end up?

Paranormal romance fantasies are incredibly popular and sales show no signs of slowing. Readers want to dream about heroes who are incredibly hot, sexy, and strong, and who also happen to come with an edge tempered by a good soul. Guys with supernatural abilities, both strength and wits, would make exceptional partners, wouldn't they? Now toss in another factor, that this amazing supernatural guy has the hots for you and only you, loves you as a soul mate, has never loved anyone with this intensity before, and so forth, and you have the makings of a sizzling read.

Paranormal characters are the ultimate lovers, whether they're werewolves, vampires, ghosts, faeries, or, of course, Shadowhunters with angel blood. Jace literally *glows* at the end of *City of Lost Souls.*

But paranormal romance novels offer more than sexy guys. Shape-shifting heroines may represent our struggles with body image or even emotional stability. Vampires such as Camille Belcourt and Will Herondale have the allure of immortality, as do warlocks such as Magnus Bane. There's a certain charm to Camille, nasty as she can be; she's gorgeous, sexy, and smart, and she can live forever if conditions are right. Of course, if conditions are wrong, she can die, as she does in *City of Lost Souls,* which personally saddens me because I like Camille as a villain. One of the unique features of this series is that Cassandra Clare's vampires *can* die if another vampire drains all the blood from their body.

Character and story development are paramount in good paranormal romances. In our sometimes bleak world, it's nice to think that good can beat evil, that love can predominate and smother hatred and other ill will. Readers get lost in the interesting settings and enthralled by the cast of supernatural characters. It's fun to read about Shadowhunters and angels, it's wonderful when they beat pure evil like Valentine, Sebastian, Lilith, and Mortmain. It makes us realize that perhaps our own problems aren't as horrible as we thought, at least for the time while we're deep in the otherworld with our fantasy characters. Readers go wild for a series, the more novels the better, when they fall in love with characters such as Clary, Jace, Will, and Tessa. We can't wait for the next book. We want their lives to turn out well, we want them to live happily ever after, but on the other hand, we're not ready to say good-bye to them yet. Paranormals have the deep attraction of traditional soap operas in this regard, where in the old days women watched their favorite characters fives days per week, sometimes for decades.

Perhaps teens are drawn to paranormals because they grew up with Harry Potter novels. Perhaps they like the idea of having special powers like Clary and Tessa, of attracting hotties like Jace and Will. It's always about wish fulfillment, where lovers overcome incredible obstacles to finally find true love with each other. Who doesn't want a soul mate? When you jigger in magic spells, demon blood, demons, ghosts, and other supernatural elements, love and sex become fraught with obstacles, dangers, and mysteries—and the sexual tension tightens dramatically. Everything becomes more exciting. A paranormal romance couple must overcome obstacles the normal human couple couldn't even imagine, and that's the beauty of the genre.

So what's the fundamental aspect of writing romance novels? Maybe it's that the story must focus on a developing relationship between lovers. If you pulled the romance out of the book, the entire story would collapse, and there wouldn't be enough substance left to keep readers interested. This is true in The Mortal Instruments, where the developing love relationship between Clary and Jace consumes a huge amount of story time. If you removed their romance from the novels, the books would fall flat. Now, it is true that even without the romance, these novels would still have fully developed fantasy-adventure plots. The books wouldn't be as interesting, but they'd still function as paranormal fantasies. So basically, it's my take that these are paranormal fantasies with heavy overtones of romance. Again, this is part of the reason I believe Cassandra Clare has done a remarkable job with these novels. It's not easy to write five-hundred-page novels, one after the other after the other, with sixty characters or more and multiple romantic relationships layered onto complex character and plot development. I've written twenty-seven books and sixty short stories, and trust me, what Cassandra Clare has done—and continues to do—is not a simple task.

Let's move on to the heart of things, so to speak. Let's have a little fun with some of the major romances in these books.

First we'll talk about romantic triangles, which are abundant in these novels, and explore why they help move the action forward.

ROMANTIC TRIANGLES

We've seen romantic triangles in everything from Twilight to The Hunger Games, and now in both The Mortal Instruments and The Infernal Devices. This is a popular device in romance novels and other media such as film and television. If the protagonist is torn between a really hot guy and her male best friend, the emotional tension is heightened. Will she choose her best friend, who's always been there for her and makes her laugh, who's the sweetest guy possible? Or will she choose the sexy one who may not be as sweet on the surface? The sexy guy may be harder with deeper angst. He may not understand his own emotions and why he's so attracted to her, and so he may not treat her as well as her male best friend. Or he might be great, but it just so happens he's supernatural. Maybe he's a bad boy who has to be brought out of his shell. There are a lot of reasons and motivations in fiction, and these are only a small sample of how an author can use characters to build romantic tension.

In Stephenie Meyer's *Twilight*, Bella Swan is in love with vampire Edward Cullen, and when he leaves her in *New Moon* to protect her life, she becomes extremely good friends with werewolf Jacob Black. At the end of *Eclipse*, she chooses to marry Edward instead of Jacob. For readers, *New Moon* and *Eclipse* heighten the romantic tension between Bella and Edward because we worry that she might not end up with Edward. (Yes, I know that I'm writing from the perspective of Team Edward. If you flip what I just wrote, you see that the same idea could apply to the bond between Bella and Jacob. For readers who were rooting for Jacob, Bella's relationship with Edward only heightens the tension.)

Another example might come from Suzanne Collins's The Hunger Games, in which Katniss Everdeen is drawn to both Peeta Mellark and Gale Hawthorne. This series of books has a romantic angle and, indeed, a romantic triangle. In this case, Gale is the boy with the harder edge. He's a woodsman, a hunter like Katniss, and they've been best friends since childhood. Peeta's the sweet, softer one. Katniss resists him for a long time, though you have to factor in that they're fighting to the death under extreme circumstances. It's not the optimum way to get to know somebody romantically. However, the romantic tension is evident throughout the series, and Katniss ends up marrying Peeta.

I recently rewatched the entire run of *Gossip Girl,* which some of you might remember from either the books or the television program. I read all the books when they came out years ago but only recently decided to watch all the shows in order. In this case, Blair Waldorf's best male friend since childhood is Nate Archibald. She's in love with him forever, it seems, but ends up with Chuck Bass, another longtime friend. Her female best friend, Serena van der Woodsen, is in a love triangle with Blair and Nate for a while, which is a large factor in Blair's decision to end her romance with Nate. As with all fictional triangles, readers and viewers feel attached to the series; they're drawn to it because of the heightened romantic tension created by the love triangles. Along with a lot of other reasons for liking a fictional series, fans want their favorite characters—Bella, Katniss, Blair—to choose the right guy.

Cassandra Clare knows how to use this technique very well. Among the many romantic triangles in The Mortal Instruments and The Infernal Devices are the relationships among Clary, Jace, and Simon (and if you include the brief interlude with pseudo-Sebastian, it's temporarily a quadrangle); Jocelyn, Valentine, and Luke; Simon, Isabelle, and Maia; Maia, Simon, and Jordan; and Tessa, William, and Jem.

In The Mortal Instruments, best friend Simon is so jealous of Jace that he finally admits to Clary that he's been in love with her for many years. She's unable to say the same in return and, in fact, is stunned by his revelation. However, as with all carefully drawn protagonists, Clary feels conflicted, perhaps even guilty and emotionally distraught that she can't say the same thing. This is often true in the real world, when a girl's best male friend professes romantic love for her, and she just can't return the feelings. She doesn't want to lose her friend, she doesn't want to hurt his feelings, yet her heart belongs somewhere else (or perhaps she doesn't feel love for anyone else, but she knows that she's not *in love* with her friend). Clary is in this same situation, and she worries about what she would really say if she had to tell Simon the truth.

Clary even dreams about both Jace and Simon at the same time. In an early dream, she's dancing with Simon in a romantic setting complete with champagne fountains and gold everywhere. Suddenly, Jace is with her instead, and as the subconscious often does for us in the real world, in her dream, her feelings stir for Jace in ways she doesn't quite understand. This is the author's way of showing us that Clary's feeling are blossoming for Jace instead of Simon.

In Clary's case, things become much more complicated because for a long time she and Jace think that they are sister and brother. This factor really jacks up the romantic tension, which I'll talk about later in this chapter. Like real people who get flustered and blurt things out, both she and Jace are constantly tormented by the sister-brother dilemma, professing love for each other despite it and then trying to remain cool and distance themselves from each other. Of course, let's hope that real people who get flustered and blurt things out aren't potential sister-brother lovers! Anyway, I knew that Clary must end up with Jace, and I knew that he couldn't really be her brother because romantically they belong together. I also knew that Simon wouldn't quite cut it as a romantic figure for Clary, even when Simon becomes a much sexier dude later, a vampire with great skill, bravery, and that extra sheen that vampires physically obtain. Cassandra Clare casts Simon later as a developing romantic figure, but not for Clary. Rather, the author develops him as a nice guy who ends up confused romantically and not really knowing how to handle his own conflicted emotions. Indeed, Simon finds himself in his own romantic triangle with Isabelle and Maia, which I'll talk about briefly in a minute.

This is often how it is in real life, where physical attraction and chemistry are mysteries to us. Why do we prefer a new guy romantically instead of one we've known our whole lives? Why does his hand feel different to us, and somehow magical? We all puzzle through feelings such as these, and in fiction, romantic triangles such as the one with Clary, Jace, and Simon dramatize our real-world dilemmas and emotional dilemmas.

In an interesting move, Cassandra Clare develops a similar romantic triangle with Clary's mother, Jocelyn Fray, her father Valentine Morgenstern, and Jocelyn's best male friend, Luke

Galloway. Jocelyn and Luke's relationship reminds me of the one Clary has with Simon. Both Luke and Simon are incredibly faithful friends, who stick loyally by the females they love despite the fact that Clary and Jocelyn are not really in love with them. (Jocelyn eventually realizes that she loves Luke and marries him, but it takes her decades to reach this decision.) In this way, fiction differs from reality, in which no guy with an ego of any kind will remain with a girl for decades (or throughout high school or college), madly in love with her, doing everything he can for her and her daughter (if she has one, as is the case with the adult Jocelyn), while never professing his true love for her, especially with another guy marrying her, having sex with her, and claiming her as his own. In the real world, people suffer too much if they're in love with somebody who can't return their feelings. Friendship is one thing; being madly in love with somebody is quite another. Once the line is crossed, once a guy professes true love to a girl, if she doesn't return his feelings, he must stifle his love and move on—in the real world—or the friendship suffers. In fiction, authors can bend rules to create dramatic tension, in this case, of a romantic nature. Luke stays with Jocelyn forever like a faithful lapdog—or lap wolf, as the case may be—dating nobody else, marrying nobody else, in love with Jocelyn but not telling her about it for many years. In the meantime, like Clary with Jace, Jocelyn's true love went to the evil Valentine, her husband from long ago. Sure, she's no longer in love with Valentine, and hence there's no emotional struggle involved. She's not torn between the evil Valentine and the nice Luke. Jocelyn's all grown up, and let's face it, Valentine's too much of a bad boy for any real woman to love. Still, the love triangle of girl–bad boy–good boy is there, isn't it? You might argue that Jace isn't really a bad boy because, after all, he does transform into an angelic being later, but compared to

Simon, Jace definitely has *edge*, which romantically translates into *sexy*.

GIRL	BAD BOY	GOOD BOY
Clary	Jace (bad boy in a good way)	Simon
Jocelyn	Valentine (bad boy in a very bad way)	Luke

What do *you* think?

Then there's dear old Simon, who's caught in a love triangle with Clary and Jace. Eventually, he creates romantic problems of an entirely different nature for himself, similar to problems people encounter in real life. To show us (rather than tell us) that Simon is becoming more sexually appealing, Cassandra Clare dishes up a relationship between Simon and the sexy Isabelle. You might remember that Clary is often jealous of Isabelle's physical appearance, viewing her as prettier and sexier than herself. So when Isabelle starts a romantic relationship with Simon, it's the author's way of showing not only that Simon is indeed appealing but also that Clary has two romantic choices, one in Jace, the other in Simon, whom I viewed originally—for example, in the opening scenes in the Pandemonium Club of *City of Bones*—as responsible and somewhat nerdy.

In *City of Fallen Angels,* the author shows us how attractive Isabelle Lightwood is from Simon's point of view. Isabelle always wears extremely sexy clothes and draws the attention of boys wherever she goes. Her beauty and sexiness are defined very clearly throughout these novels. Here, Simon—as is the case with many responsible-nerdy guys in the real world who end up dating extremely sexy girls—is amazed that Isabelle is paying any attention to him whatsoever. The author shows us further that Clary has dismissed Simon as a romantic option when she writes that Clary finds it extremely amusing that he's dating Isabelle. But he's two-timing Isabelle, isn't he? Because he's also dating werewolf Maia Roberts, when Clary's mother, Jocelyn, marries werewolf Luke Garroway aka Lucian Graymark, and Simon must choose to bring one of his girlfriends to the wedding and hurt the other. Simon must break his romantic triangle. This is hard for him because in general Simon is such a nice person.

So why do boys date two girls at once? Why do these romantic triangles exist in the first place—that is, in the real world? The short answer is that sometimes people can't decide if they like the characteristics of one person more than the traits of another person. What one person has, the other lacks. This is certainly true of Simon, who tells Jordan Kyle that the two girls appeal to him for very different reasons. As Clary likes Simon because he is mature and responsible, Simon likes Maia because she's down-to-earth and laid-back. As Clary likes Jace because he excites her, Simon likes Isabelle because she's sexy and excites him. These novels contain many romantic parallels, and I'm describing only a few.

In addition, the romantic triangles overlap and ripple from one to the other, and then to yet another. So in this case, Jordan Kyle becomes involved with Maia Roberts, who then must puzzle through her conflicting emotions about Simon and Jordan. Another triangle starts forming with Maia, Simon, and Jordan, and then to complicate romantic matters further, Isabelle catches Simon two-timing her and he must then chase Isabelle to win her love. But the overlapping goes on and on, which is one way Cassandra Clare keeps us hooked and guessing about who will end up with whom. You see, it turns out that Jordan used to be with Maia long ago, and he never stopped loving her, yet for them to be together requires that she forgive him for turning her into a werewolf back then. That's a bit much to forgive, isn't it? But on the other hand, we think as readers, they have a lot in common, given that they're both werewolves.

There's one more romantic triangle I want to cover in this section before moving on. Trust me, I could analyze these romantic triangles endlessly, they're that complex and overlapping. If you're interested in taking these thoughts further, you should try writing your own essay about one aspect of all of the above, such as why Simon starts dating two girls simultaneously and why he can't bring himself to choose just one.

But I can't dismiss this triangle subject without mentioning Tessa Gray with William Herondale and Jem aka James Carstairs, as this is a huge romantic situation in The Infernal Devices. In this case, Will and Jem are parabatai, which means they're soul brothers for life. They have an unbreakable bond, which makes the romantic tension acute when both of them fall for Tessa. How can she choose between them? She kisses Jem in many scenes, and he professes his love for her in many ways throughout The Infernal Devices. As is the case with girls who have male best friends in the real world, Tessa feels that Jem truly understands her, that she can let him see her true self. This is the stamp of a good friend but not always the key to romance. She misses him, too, but again, this is the stamp of friendship and not necessarily romance. On the other hand, the excitement she feels with Will reminds me of the excitement that Clary feels with Jace.

As Clary has Simon and as Simon has Maia, Tessa has Jem. As Clary has Jace and as Simon has Isabelle, Tessa has Will. These are the parallels as I see them.

Many of us, including Tessa, wonder whether it's possible to love more than one person at once. Sometimes it's confusing. What's love versus deep friendship? How can Tessa truly know the difference? It is for this reason that readers are glued to these books. At some point in our own lives, we all face these types of questions, and watching Cassandra Clare's characters work through these issues helps us understand our own emotions and reactions to them.

KEY ROMANCES

The huge romance in The Mortal Instruments series, books one through five, anyway, is the one between Clary and Jace. So let's chat about that relationship first and then tackle some of the other key romances as well.

Clary and Jace

What attracts them to each other and what brings them together in the first place? What obstacles do they face in their romance; that is, what keeps these lovers apart and makes us turn pages to learn the outcome? Does Cassandra Clare offer clues about their sibling relationship? How realistic is their relationship?

Jace is Clary's "golden boy" from the first moment she sees him. Her first reaction to Jace is that he reminds her of a lion. It's in his expressions and movements, almost as if he's constantly on the lookout for danger as well as for those he hunts. This is an interesting way of introducing the main hero of The Mortal Instruments series. Lions are gold and tawny; they rule as King of the Jungle. So by using this analogy, Cassandra Clare lets us know that Jace is going to be a central figure, a leader and hero on some level.

In addition, we figure he's on the side of good rather than being a leader of the villains, for example, because Cassandra Clare has Jace swear "By the Angel" right away in response to a reference to "Infernal Worlds." Well, angels are typically good, while anything infernal is typically not so great.

For me, the next *huge* clue that Jace is going to become Clary's golden boy is when, like a lion in the jungle, he quickly and cleanly stabs the blue-haired demon boy in the Pandemonium Club, who disappears into thin air. It is at this point that we clearly realize that these books are about the supernatural. Besides, Jace keeps calling Clary a mundane. Anybody in traditional science-fiction and fantasy (SFF) fandom knows that we've called those who aren't into SFF "mundanes" for decades. I love this little play on the word *mundane* in The Mortal Instruments.

Jace's place as golden boy is underscored further when Clary thinks about his "tawny eyes," and we soon know this guy is heading down that long fictional road toward being her soul mate. For the first time, we see the faint lines of runes on his bare arms, the cocky twist of his mouth. Only edgy guys with attitudes look at heroines in this way, oh and lest we forget, he's tough as all hell with his wide metal cuffs and knife. Cassandra Clare has already set things up so we can't wait for the moment when Clary realizes that she has the hots for Jace.

This moment starts gelling when Clary develops a soft spot for him, realizing that Jace must be lonely. When she asks him if he has friends other than Alec, Isabelle, and Max, Jace pauses, stops stroking Church the cat, and answers with a simple yes. Because of this pause and simple reaction, we as readers know that Jace is lonely, and so does Clary. But in classic tough guy romance form, Jace cuts the conversation short and claims he doesn't need anything else, and that's that. We know that he plays it "close to the chest" in true tough-guy manner, and at this stage of the story, he doesn't let his feelings show very easily. At this point, we know that if and when Clary falls for this guy, she's going to fall fast and hard.

The witch Madame Dorothea foreshadows this great romance when she reads Jace's tea leaves and tells him that he's going to fall in love, but with the wrong person. And then, just as predicted, of course, Clary draws the Ace of Cups from Dorothea's tarot cards, and yes, it's the card of love. This foreshadowing follows what every writer knows (or should know): you don't put a loaded gun in a room if you don't intend to use it. In this case, you don't foreshadow love through tarot cards unless you intend to have the characters fall in love. When Madame Dorothea indicates that Jace will fall in love with the wrong person, it maintains the suspense about their supposed sister-brother relationship. We learn much later that the tarot cards, which Jocelyn painted, have a very special meaning in this story, so for me, the fact that Clary draws the Ace of Cups from this particular deck means it is almost *fated* that Clary will fall in love with Jace. For me, this is a huge symbol of what will come.

In true romantic form, Cassandra Clare lets her lovers take their time. She lets their attraction grow, and it's nearly three hundred pages into the story when she tells us that Clary feels "the hard muscles of his abdomen" when he "jammed the point of the stele into the ignition" (*City of Bones,* page 288). If this isn't a sexual innuendo, well, what is? And by the way, that they happen to be on a supernatural motorcycle doesn't exactly detract from the vision of Jace as a sexy guy.

After setting up Jace as physically strong and wisecracking, the author mellows him out a little, too, and shows Jace to be a really nice guy. For example, he treats Clary to a birthday surprise and gives her a witchlight rune-stone. We see that he cares about her and is genuinely fond of her, which for readers means that we wouldn't mind being with this kind of guy, either. The author wants us to like Jace and root for him. The romantic aspects of these books are incredibly well done.

Okay, so he's sexy, he's tough, he's smart, and he's nice. Something must happen now to get the sizzle going and the flames erupting. The attraction is there on all levels. By page 315 of *City of Bones,* they're kissing, and on page 317, well, they're kissing again. Clary's heart beats fast—and often—she melts into him, he says all the right things, such as "all I could think about was you" (*City of Bones,* page 363). We're in full romance mode now.

Given that these novels are epic fantasies as well as romantic, Jace must also save her life a few times, which he does, and he must tell her that he loves her, which he also does.

Every good epic romance needs a huge obstacle placed squarely between the lovers, for without choices and dilemmas, we can't have a good story, right? In The Mortal Instruments, the author gives us a biggie. Anyone who's read these novels instantly knows what I mean, and besides, I've already mentioned this one huge obstacle a couple of times.

Just for fun, here are some choices for the one huge obstacle:

1. **Clary and Jace can't live in the same town.**
2. **Clary and Jace argue too much and about too many things.**
3. **Clary actually loves Magnus Bane.**
4. **Clary and Jace think they're sister and brother.**

Obviously, you must have correctly guessed number 4, that they think they're brother and sister. If this factor doesn't make you turn the pages, dying to know how they get together in the end, I don't know what would. It was clear to me that Cassandra Clare would indeed fix this problem for her two star-crossed lovers. I assumed right away that Valentine could not be Jace's father, that Jace would discover the identity of his true father at some point, so he could be with Clary.

Cassandra Clare offers plenty of clues that they are *not* really brother and sister. For one thing, the desire between them is incredibly strong, and should it turn out that they are siblings, their love affair would fall in the category of incest. It seemed highly unlikely to me—impossible, in fact—that the author would feature such a relationship as the primary romance in an epic series of paranormal fantasy novels. But even setting this real-world consideration aside, that an author wouldn't feature incest as the huge romance in a series about teenagers—there *are* other big clues.

For example, the Queen of Faeries says that a kiss will set Clary free. When Clary asks the queen if she wants Jace to kiss *her,* we figure that Clary is being naïve. We guess that the queen is referring to Jace kissing Clary. In typical Simon fashion, jealous and protecting Clary with the determination of a tigre, he's not too happy when the Queen of Faeries emphasizes that the kiss is the one that Clary desires the most. Following this scene are streams of romantic pages, one after the other, about desire, Jace kissing Clary, Clary loving Jace, and Jace loving Clary.

The next clue comes when Amatis tells Clary that she looks like Jocelyn whereas Jace looks like Valentine. This makes us think that perhaps the two lovers aren't so star-crossed, after all. Perhaps they do indeed have different fathers. Of course, we're supposed to wonder if Jace's father is Valentine rather than Clary's father, but you see, for me, the big clue is that Amatis emphasizes that Clary looks like Jocelyn. For me, this strongly sets up that Clary looks like her *mother,* not her father. Amatis does not tell Clary that she has her father's eyes and hair but her mother's body shape, or that Clary has Valentine's nose and lips and profile but her mother's skin type. As it turns out, of course, Valentine is indeed Clary's father, not Jace's father, reminding me of the piles of mystery novels I read as a teenager. The authors always placed clues that led us readers down the wrong paths. While I deduced correctly that Clary and Jace aren't sister and brother, it could have been tricky to guess from the clues which one of them had the grotesque fortune of having Valentine as a father. Kudos to Cassandra Clare for planting seeds of mystery.

It almost feels like an endless on-off-on-off binary sequence, as Clary and Jace profess great love, then back away, then do it all over again. So much drama, and what a tumultuous relationship, ramping up the romantic tension. You see, they simply *can't* be together, right?

But we, the readers, know that they *will* be together.

Because there's no way for this obstacle to remain in their path. It must fall down. Anything less, after all these two characters have suffered, would be torture. The books would end as tragedies rather than romances.

Of course, in the end, we do indeed discover the identity of Jace's father and we learn that Clary and Jace aren't siblings.

But there's another obstacle confronting these two lovers. In *City of Fallen Angels,* Jace has terrible nightmares about Clary and fears that he might hurt her. So instead of telling her the truth, he avoids her, says he can't talk to her, and he goes to the extreme of not even looking at her at times. I'm not sure why he doesn't just tell her the truth about his nightmares, but he doesn't.

Finally, Clary decides that something must be behind Jace's nightmares, and to solve the obstacle of the nightmare in their romance, Clary must learn who planted the nightmares into Jace's mind. What demonic influence possesses him? How can she strip it off?

If ever there was a need for a love triangle, *City of Fallen Angels* provides a killer motivation. Demonic influence Lilith explains on page 339 that, for Sebastian to return to the dark forces, she requires that both Jace and Simon be present. So

Lilith uses Clary as a lure, a catalyst, to bring both boys who love Clary—both Jace and Simon—to Lilith's den. The original triangle must exist (Clary, Jace, and Simon) for this plot device to work.

How realistic is their relationship? Here's what I think. It all makes sense and works for me except for one thing, and I bet you can guess what I mean. In my real world, there is no way I could have huge romantic thoughts about, much less make out with (kiss, etc.), somebody I thought was my own brother. As soon as I thought I had evidence that some guy was really my brother by blood, trust me, there's no way I'd continue to have any romantic inclinations toward him. It would all die—*poof!*—just like that. The fact that Jace continues to have the hots for Clary is a stretch for me. One of them still boiling for the other sexually is a stretch, but both of them still feeling this way is an enormous stretch.

I grant that the author gets around the problem in a very clever way. After all, I don't have angel blood or demon blood, I'm not supernatural in any way. Perhaps the blood does indeed bind Clary and Jace, but not in a sibling sense, rather in a powerful, physical fashion that they simply cannot ignore. Perhaps the fact that they're both supernatural angelic forces created by Valentine's evil demonic experiments seals their fate to be together. If all of this is the case—and only Cassandra Clare has the answer (along with perhaps her agent and editor)—and most important, if our soul mates are determined by fate, then any relationship becomes realistic.

Clary and Simon

Clary and Simon don't really have a romantic relationship. They're best friends with the caveat that Simon's in love with her, which makes their relationship pseudoromantic, I suppose.

Of course, when other girls find Simon attractive, it raises Simon's stock in the eyes of readers. And by raising his stock, it also raises Clary's, because—speaking in fictional generalities—it's easier to admire a heroine if the boys who have the hots for her are attractive rather than supernerdy.

But there's no doubt that Clary truly loves Simon as a friend, almost as if he's a brother. When Simon turns literally into a rat, Clary does everything she can to restore him to human form.

When Simon kisses her, Clary doesn't push him away, and she even lets herself reflect upon the similarities and differences between Simon's kisses and Jace's. The only thing that interrupts this romantic foreplay is the telephone ringing, so it's not as if Simon is some loser for whom Clary doesn't lust.

But when Clary and Simon kiss again, and Simon goes as far as to tell her that he loves her, Clary finds herself thinking about Jace. This instant reaction is what happens quite often in real life, when someone professes love for a person who is already in love with somebody else. The mind flashes to the loved one. Although Clary tries to force herself not to remember how it felt to kiss Jace, her body remembers. We all know what that's like, when our bodies react as if not under the control of our minds. In short, this is what we call romantic "chemistry."

The relationship evolves alongside Clary's on-and-off brother-sister-lover-friend relationship with Jace. Throughout it all, Simon remains in love with Clary, steadfast and reliable. Romance novels work very well when the heroine has an edgy macho lover like Jace but also a best-friend-forever-loves-her-forever guy like Simon. It enables the heroine to analyze each personality in light of the other and to eventually realize what true love really means and whom she really wants. By comparing and contrasting her feelings for Simon, even the kisses, Clary is able to cope with and finally understand her feelings for Jace.

What keeps Clary and Simon apart as lovers? Just what is the obstacle *they* must overcome? Can you guess?

It's Clary's heart. Even if she'd never met Jace, I doubt she would have fallen deeply in love with Simon.

Their relationship is certainly a common one in fictional romance. Think about the love triangle of Dan Humphrey, Serena van der Woodsen, and Vanessa Abrams in *Gossip Girl*. Vanessa is Dan's former girlfriend and remains his best friend for an extremely long time, just like Simon remains Clary's best friend. For a long time, Vanessa seems to stick by Dan and love him as a sibling, just as Simon does for Clary.

Dan's friendship feelings for Vanessa help him understand his attraction to Serena. Clary's friendship feelings for Simon help her understand her attraction to Jace.

Frankly, I've lost track of how many guys Serena falls in love with during the course of the entire *Gossip Girl* series, but after a constant on-again, off-again romance with Dan Humphrey, she ends up friends with him but not lovers. Vanessa then steps in to become Dan's lover again, not due to her own initiation but rather because they have a threesome with a movie star, and Dan realizes that he's still in love with Vanessa. In the end, things flip again, and Serena and Dan end up together despite the fact that *he* is supposedly Gossip Girl. In this manner, the Dan-Vanessa-Serena love triangle differs a lot from the Clary-Jace-Simon triangle.

But circling back, is Clary and Simon's relationship realistic? Is it possible to love a boyfriend without having romantic feelings? Of course it is. We all have good friends of the opposite sex. Remember Peeta Mellark in The Hunger Games? Katniss Everdeen considered him a friend and *only* a friend for a very long time, yet she ended up with him in the end. Had Clary ended up with Simon in the end, it would have felt a lot like Katniss and Peeta. I was worrying that Cassandra Clare might choose this option, but I figured the epic fantasy structure would lead her to keep Jace as Clary's soul mate. But Clary and Simon's relationship does make sense to me. The only part of it that feels "off" is that Simon continues to be in love with her for much longer than a real guy would maintain the faith. Most guys would shrug off the love aspect long before Simon. Male ego and self-respect would make sure of it. Not to be sexist; a girl wouldn't sit around being steadfast in this type of situation, either. As with male ego, girls usually have sufficient self-respect to move past a doomed romance.

Clary and Sebastian

In a stunning turn of events, Clary and Sebastian embark on a brief romance and actually kiss. Of course, throughout this brief attraction, just as most girls would do in these circumstances, Clary thinks about Jace a lot. But what attracts her to Sebastian in the first place? Does he remind her of Jace?

For one thing, he isn't *really* Sebastian Verlac—he's her blood brother, Jonathan Christopher Morgenstern—and he's very nice to her in the beginning, which is probably why she starts falling for him. When you can't be with someone you love, sometimes you're so discouraged about it that you fall prey to someone else.

The main obstacle Clary and the false Sebastian face in terms of romance is that he's an imposter, not really Sebastian at all. *He's her brother.* Her description of the false Sebastian later doesn't make him sound very attractive. She tells Luke that the imposter has poorly dyed hair, among other things. As for any romance between Clary and Sebastian Verlac aka Jonathan Christopher Morgenstern, forget it. He's much too evil and doesn't understand family relationships and their boundaries. Clary doesn't make the mistake her mother made with Valentine. Luckily, Clary knows evil when she sees it, even before we learn that Sebastian is actually her brother. Of course, Valentine was supposedly not so bad in the beginning of his romance with Jocelyn, but still, Clary has some smarts when it comes to choosing her men.

Simon and Isabelle

These two come together initially because Isabelle likes to date boys her parents disapprove of, and Simon happens to be a vampire. In Isabelle's Shadowhunter world, all Downworlder dates are off-limits. When parents disapprove of boys in the real world, does this make them more appealing to girls? I suppose this is true for some girls and not for others. It depends on the girl's personality and also on her relationship with her parents.

Simon and Isabelle's relationship begins as friendship, then advances to dating. However, Isabelle claims that Simon is too sweet and boring for her and later confesses that she said these sorts of things only because she's always known that Simon is in love with Clary. In the real world, girls don't want to give their hearts to boys who are in love with somebody else, so it makes sense that Isabelle feels this way.

However, over time, they do fall in love, and eventually Simon bites Isabelle. When Isabelle doesn't start transforming into a vampire, we wonder if and when this will happen in the sixth book of the series. As for Simon, he's pleasantly surprised when she gets pleasure from the bite, possibly setting things up for a more romantic relationship. Whether they continue to go down the path of intense romance remains to be seen.

Maia and Jordan Kyle

As a paranormal fantasy reader, if you like romances between supernatural creatures, The Mortal Instruments gives you plenty of choices. In this case, the author explores what would happen between a werewolf boyfriend and the girl he bites. If that weren't enough to agitate a girl, imagine if the boyfriend then leaves her, which is what Jordan Kyle does to Maia. This would be enough to upset any girl, and in true fashion, Maia holds it against him for a very long time. If after such an extended period, this werewolf boyfriend should show up professing his love for the girl, it would still take some time for her to believe him. But what if the bad boy has become a Good Samaritan? It might take a while, but it's conceivable that the girl, such as Maia, would finally forgive the boy, such as Jordan. The fact that Jordan becomes such a doer of good makes us believe that he can win her heart again.

Mostly, with Jordan, I wonder how he affords to live in New York City on a bike messenger's salary. He buys fancy televisions and video games, and he lives quite well. I also find it amazing that he has enough money to offer to pay for Maia's Stanford University tuition. Cassandra Clare provides the answer when she tells us that Jordan saved the money from his Praetor income. His salary must be through the roof! I guess it pays to work for a werewolf company.

Magnus Bane and Alec

These days, it's considered PC, or politically correct, to insert gay lovers in novels. Some authors do it just to gain audience, but I don't think that's the case with Magnus Bane and Alec Lightwood. I think they're one of the most fun couples in The Mortal Instruments.

Alec has troubles typical for gay people in our real world, worrying how people will react to his sexual preferences, and he hides the fact that he's gay for as long as he can get away with it. He worries about his parents' reaction, as well as Jace's, for whom he has the hots. Our society's attitudes are reflected in discussions, such as the one when Alec wonders if Simon is threatening to expose the fact that he's gay.

The romance in The Mortal Instruments between warlock Magnus Bane and Shadowhunter Alec is almost epic in proportions, and for me, is a highlight of the series. This might be due to the fact that Magnus Bane is one of my favorite characters. Or perhaps it's because the author forces us to think about our own morals and ethics. After all, the relationship between Magnus and Alec revolves around issues of trust, jealousy, and the extremes we go to due to lack of self-confidence; it's about forgiveness, and the implications of just pushing our loved ones too far.

Driven nearly mad by jealousy, however, Alec makes a big mistake, an interesting one that adds a lot of dimension to both his character and that of Magnus Bane. Because he can't bear that Magnus and the immortal vampire Camille were once lovers, he asks Camille to magically take away Magnus's immortality. Acting very selfishly, Alec figures he and Magnus can grow old together.

How can Alec betray Magnus in such a major way and yet expect love in return? What is he thinking? Obviously, it's a huge betrayal, and when Magnus learns about it, the romance ends. Sometimes, if you want something too badly, you destroy any chance of having it.

Was Magnus wrong to end his romance with Alec? What do you think? I would have done the same thing. You can't trust a lover who's willing to take away your actual life.

Jocelyn and Valentine

A terrible romance if ever there was one, Jocelyn falls in love with Valentine, only to discover much later that he's evil.

When he dopes her during pregnancy to experiment on their unborn child, hoping to create a class of superwarriors in Nazi style, Jocelyn sees what he really is. What takes her so long? How did she not know that Valentine was such a horrible man?

But it does take her a long time, and before the ugly truth hits, she actually loves Valentine. I'm not sure what she sees in him, to be honest. Anyone as evil as Valentine is going to slip up and give himself away from time to time. His wife would find clues that he's up to no good, that he isn't who he pretends to be. When Jocelyn finally discovers his lab notebooks, that he was torturing and killing all sorts of creatures, that he wanted to kill all the Downworlders, she turns to Luke Garroway and leaves the Circle. But it sure takes her a long time, doesn't it?

Jocelyn and Luke

What took Jocelyn so long—a decade and a half—to finally accept love with Luke, and what took Luke so long to tell her that he loved her? This is a relationship that baffles me. Given that Luke is so steadfast and loyal, helping Jocelyn in every way over the years and serving as a father figure to Clary, there's no way that Jocelyn could possibly *not* know that this guy's in love with her. I would know. Wouldn't you?

Long ago, Lucian Graymark aka Luke Garroway was Valentine's second in command, not to mention the best man at Jocelyn and Valentine's wedding. In fact, they all grew up together.

Even at the wedding, Cassandra Clare drops hints for the reader that Luke's always been in love with Jocelyn and that she's always really known it—deep inside her heart, she's known it, but for some reason it's never surfaced. At the wedding, all the clues are there, including depressed looks on his face, the fact that should Valentine not show up, she would have to marry the best man, and Jocelyn even teases Luke about marrying her.

Personally, I think that Luke would have offered to marry Jocelyn when Clary was still a young girl, and that Jocelyn would have said yes—that is, if these were real people in our real world. Single mother, single man, alone forever, never dating anybody else; what took them so long?

Given how far back these characters go together and how well they've always known each other, I wonder how much Luke knew about the experiments Valentine performed on his pregnant wife. I also wonder how Luke could not have foreseen, at least to some extent, how evil his best friend would become.

Tessa and William

The relationship between Tessa and William reminds me of the one between Clary and Jace. Will has Jace's edge, veneer of ego, and sense of humor. Like Jace, Will is the bad boy who's really good. He jokes around and leads Tessa on in the beginning, and she's attracted to him very early on. He's also attracted to her very early on. In addition, Tessa and William have an on-again, off-again romance, where he's drawn to her but keeps pulling back. All of these factors are the same as with Clary and Jace.

Do you remember when Jace pushes Clary away because he has nightmares about killing her? In a similar manner, Will pushes Tessa away because he thinks he's cursed and anyone he loves will die. Will goes so far as to ask Old Mol for a potion that will make him indifferent to Tessa—out of fear that his love for her will kill her.

Another similarity is that each girl notices that other girls find their guys attractive. It's made very clear that basically no girl can resist Jace, which probably makes Jace even sexier to

Clary. Tessa notices that Bridget thinks Will is hot, which probably makes Will even more alluring to Tessa.

But there's more to the Tessa-Will romance than pure physical attraction. It turns out that Will is kind and romantic in his actions. For example, he leaves a book for her because he knows she will enjoy it. He also writes a poem for her. Tessa notes that Will always makes her laugh, and all girls know that this is a good attribute to have in your guy.

So what keeps these two lovers apart, how do they overcome their problems (or not), and how do they end up? The main obstacle that Tessa and Will face is his fear that his love will kill her. They get past this obstacle when Will finally learns that he was never cursed to begin with. But they don't end up together by the end of *Clockwork Prince*. Instead, Tessa has agreed to marry Jem, but only because she can't bear to hurt him. Personally, I'd rather not hurt the guy I'm in love with—in Tessa's case, Will—than marry a good friend, but we'll see how all of this is resolved in future novels. It's a pretty good guess that Cassandra Clare will entertain the idea of keeping Tessa and Will together for the long haul. By the time this book is in your hands, perhaps we'll know more about their evolving relationship.

Tessa and Jem

The relationship between Tessa and Jem reminds me of the one between Clary and Simon. These two are really supposed to remain best friends, for even after Tessa agrees to marry Jem, we figure that she knows in her heart it's Will she truly wants. Tessa thinks she's an orphan, and Jem is an orphan, so they're both adrift without real family. As with Simon and Clary, Jem is always a comforting friend to Tessa. She confides in him, and he's always understanding and kind. For example, after she has problems with both her supposed brother, Nate, and with Will, it's Jem who helps her feel better.

With Will keeping his distance and switching the romance on and off, Tessa becomes increasingly dependent on Jem for even more than friendship. We're given clues that Tessa's romance with Jem will flare and cause problems for any romance between Tessa and William. For example, Jem's family ring magically fits on her finger perfectly, and they pretend to be engaged when they visit Starkweather. Pretending to be engaged or married is a good clue that these two are going to get romantically entangled possibly more than they should. When Tessa later tries to return the family ring to Jem, he says that it looks good on her, and he really prefers that she keep it. So we know that he very much wants to marry her; guys don't give their girls family rings unless they intend to have an extremely serious relationship. They kiss and hug quite a bit, she actually blushes from time to time, and she does find her heart fluttering from being romantically involved with Jem. Just like real girls in real life, Tessa's confused and torn, and she doesn't firmly know her own emotions. When push comes to shove, she can't really respond with the full intensity of love that Jem displays for her. She can't bring herself to tell him the same thing, that she's crazy in love with him; this tells us that she knows in her heart that she's really in love with William.

What keeps these two lovers apart is Tessa's clear preference for Will. She's just not in love with Jem the way she's in love with Will. Tessa and Jem, however, do end up engaged at the end of *Clockwork Prince,* but as mentioned earlier, I have my doubts as to whether Tessa will remain with Jem forever. My guess is that she'll end up with Will in future books. But only Cassandra Clare knows for sure.

Nate and Jessamine

Nate and Jessamine actually get married in a secret ceremony. The reader has doubts as to the validity of the wedding ceremony, of course, given that Nate arranged it. Earlier, thinking Nate was Tessa's real brother, Jessamine nursed him as he recovered, claiming that "men always fall in love with the woman who nurses them back to health" (*Clockwork Angel,* page 300). I'm not convinced that men always fall in love with women who nurse them back to health, for if this were the case, all hospital nurses would get dozens of marriage proposals from their patients. Apparently, Jessamine isn't a gold digger but rather wants his help in escaping the Shadowhunter life. Remember, *Clockwork Angel* and *Clockwork Prince* take place in the late 1800s, when girls didn't have many options.

Unfortunately for Jessamine, she didn't pick a good fellow to marry. Nate isn't really Tessa's brother, nor is he on the side of good. Instead, he's a force of evil and just using her. He's in Mortmain's pocket, working to help the Magister create a clockwork army and take over the world. Surely she would be tipped off that he's not what he says he is when he gets her to hide the Book of the White in Tessa's room for him. But somehow she's under his magic spell, so to speak, and she does his bidding rather than remain true to her friends and her ethics.

Of course, in real life, people who are madly in love often cannot see the horrible truth about their loved ones. We're often blind to our lovers' faults . . . until it's too late. Jessamine won't listen when anybody tries to warn her about Nate. She just keeps shrieking that they love each other.

I don't think Nate and Jessamine overcome the obstacle that keeps them from having a fully developed romance. The obstacle, that it was probably a sham wedding and he went through with it only to use her as a spy, is much too big a deal.

By the end of *Clockwork Prince,* Jessamine ends up slung across Brother Enoch's shoulder en route to the Silent City, where the Silent Brothers will attempt to extract the truth from her. And by the end of *Clockwork Prince,* Nate is dead. Not a happy couple, and not a happy ending.

4

BAD BOYS

WHO IS THE MOST EVIL?

It's always about the bad boys, isn't it? All the best epic fantasy stories feature good guys with superamazing skills battling the most horrible bad boys in the universe. Readers expect the good guys to win, and anything less is disappointing. We have faith in authors that they'll let the good guys win no matter how desperate the situation becomes. But somehow, we still worry that the good guys will be hurt, that maybe they'll die, that maybe they won't get the girl and save the world. Pitching good guys against bad boys make the story exciting, and readers can't get enough of it.

This fun little section looks at a few of the worse cases of bad boys in The Mortal Instruments and The Infernal Devices. See if you agree with my assessments!

On a scale of 1 to 10, with 1 being nice and 10 being absolutely evil, I give Valentine a 10. Anyone who kills monks or Silent Brothers is evil. In real life, if you kill somebody and steal from him, you could get life in prison or even the death sentence. I'm reminded of a real-life case in which a man was murdered at midnight for a piece of Kentucky Fried Chicken, and the murderer was sent to prison. In Valentine's case, he killed the Silent Brothers because he wanted Maellartach, the Mortal Sword. This isn't a remotely good reason to hurt anyone, much less slaughter a bunch of Silent Brothers.

Valentine's so evil he kills Downworlder children and drains them of blood. You have to be truly psychotic to harm children. So he needs their blood for the Ritual of Infernal Conversion. As with the Silent Brothers, his reason for killing children isn't remotely reasonable.

And lest we forget, Valentine chains up and starves an angel. I don't know how much worse this guy could be! His deeds are so vile that I can't rank them. Is it worse to kill monks, children, or angels? Is it worse to cut out babies from wombs? Is it worse to drug pregnant women? Everything this character does is evil. Maybe I'll revise my rating of 10 for Valentine. He flies off the scale. He gets a rating of 10 raised to the ten-millionth power.

Raphael Santiago isn't exactly a pleasant charmer, either. On a scale of 1 to 10, I give him a 9. I'd give him a 7 or 8 except that he did happen to rip out Inquisitor Aldertree's heart. This probably warrants life in prison or a death sentence in real life, too. I think of Raphael as somewhat wimpy, as well as nasty. He's the only bad boy who keeps showing up as a holographic projection instead of as his real self. I'm not quite sure how a holographic projection can rip the heart out of somebody's chest, but he manages to do it.

Then there's Benedict Lightwood, whose name even suggests that he's a traitor and a villain. How would you rate him on my evil scale of 1 to 10? He's clearly not as horrible as Valentine, but he might be on the same level as Raphael. After all, Benedict does go along with a plot to get Tessa arrested for possessing dark magic items. While he doesn't rip out anybody's heart, he does plan to give Tessa to the Magister, which would seal her fate, most likely resulting in torture even worse than what the Dark Sisters did to her. So I give him a 9.

What do you think about de Quincey? How evil is he on our scale? His music room is hell for anyone strapped in the chair onstage and tortured in front of the vampires. The fact that he pays Mrs. Black and Mrs. Dark to create a binding spell to infuse automatons with demonic energy puts de Quincey right up there on the scale, perhaps at a 9.

Then there's the opium dealer, Axel Mortmain. He's a major villain in The Infernal Devices, and also, if not for him, Jem wouldn't be an addict. On a scale of 1 to 10, I think he gets a 9, too.

But I do have another 10 in mind: Sebastian Verlac. He's a killer, just like Valentine. Remember, he murders Max and sides with Valentine in his bloody plans to kill all the Shadowhunters. If your plan is to murder an entire population, you're pure evil.

There are other bad boys in these books, of course. Of them all, which do you like the most as characters?

I'd narrow it down to Valentine and Sebastian and have a really hard time choosing which one I think is the most fun to read about. Here's the deal: Mortmain is certainly pure evil, but he doesn't have the charisma of Valentine and Sebastian. I like my villains to be evil *and* rugged. They should have all the qualities of heroes, just in reverse. I prefer them three-dimensional rather than flat, but whatever they are and how-ever well developed, for me, nothing beats bad boys with tons of charm. They're much more slimy that way.

ANGELS AND SHADOWHUNTERS

THE CREATION MYTH OF
THE MORTAL INSTRUMENTS AND
THE INFERNAL DEVICES

A central motif in the first seven novels of The Mortal Instruments and The Infernal Devices is its creation myth, which weaves the Hebrew creation myth with the Christian one and then adds a new dimension to everything. If you take The Mortal Instruments' creation myth out of the series, the plot collapses. It is that essential to the story.

Rich with symbolism, a myth reflects the beliefs and aspirations of a culture. You could almost say that a myth is like the dream of an entire people. A creation myth is their way of explaining the origin of the universe. A fancy word for this concept is *cosmogony*, which comes from two Greek words, *kosmos* (world) and *genesis* (birth). Just as children tend to be fascinated by their ancestry—that is, where they come from—cultures tend to be fascinated by their origins as well. Hence, creation myths exist in cultures all over the world.

Creation myths are intertwined symbolically with religion and even science. They reach back before the dawn of time and attempt to explain the moment of the world's birth. Scientists have yet to understand what happened at the dawn of time, and many see their religion's or culture's creation myth as symbolism of a reality we don't yet understand.

While creation myths differ somewhat around the world, they all have certain commonalities. For one, they share archetypal patterns, just as many epic fantasy stories share archetypal patterns (see chapter 2, "Spinning a Faerie Good Tale"). These patterns form a shadow myth that is a skeleton of humanity's collective dream of how order rose from chaos.

The archetypal patterns of explaining creation fall into five general categories. The first is that creation of everything rose from chaos or nothingness. The second is the idea of a primal maternal egg, a cosmic egg, from which all was born. The third suggests that everything came into existence from the relationship between a world father and a world mother. The fourth posits that a supreme creator sent an animal into the primal waters to form everything in the world from the mud. The final universal myth is that everything in our world emerged from other worlds.

The archetypal characters in these myths include a supreme creator, negative forces, the first human male and female, and the hero who symbolizes mankind's need and search for goodness, order, and new beginnings.

In The Mortal Instruments and The Infernal Devices, the main creation myth centers on the first archetypal pattern, the creation of everything rising from chaos or nothingness. Cassandra Clare references God, angels, the Devil, demons, heaven, hell, the Garden of Eden, Adam and Eve, sin, and souls. She includes all the archetypal characters, such as the supreme creator (God), the negative forces (the devil, demons), the first human male and female (Adam and Eve), and the epic heroes (Jace, Clary, Will, Tessa).

The seven current novels repeatedly emphasize the creation myth. The angels act under the guidance of God, demons are fallen angels, and a demon (Lilith) was Adam's first wife, who left the Garden of Eden. So far, this is similar to the Jewish-Christian motif.

Then the Angel Raziel created Jonathan Shadowhunter, the first of his kind—the Nephilim, to fight the demons. In our real world, people believe that the Angel Raziel knows all the secrets of the universe and transcribed these secrets in a book of magic called the Book of the Angel Raziel. This fits in with the level of power Raziel has in The Mortal Instruments, and it's also interesting to note the use of magical books such as the Gray Book, which the Angel Raziel gave to the Shadowhunters. The Gray Book is similar to the real-world concept of the Book of the Angel Raziel but pushes the concept into creative realms, where it shows the special runes that Shadowhunters cut into their skin with steles.

In The Mortal Instruments series, the Angel Raziel gave Jonathan Shadowhunter three magical tools, the Mortal Cup, the Mortal Sword, and the Mortal Mirror. Here, the tale deviates from our real world's Jewish-Christian motif, though parallels remain. For example, the Mortal Cup involves angel blood, demon blood, and human blood, just as the Christian faith emphasizes the blood of Christ.

The Shadowhunters are a fictional race created by Cassandra Clare. They aren't in the real-world Bible.

The Shadowhunter blood is magical if you consider that when automatons are smeared in it, the mechanical creatures can open the Institute's doors. Shadowhunters have other unique, God-like qualities. For example, they can see things ordinary people can't see.

Even at the opening of *City of Bones* in the Pandemonium Club, we know that Clary is special because she can see past the invisibility glamours. She has something called the Sight, which is key to her character development and to the plot of the first novel. It drives Clary's quest to discover her identity, who and what she really is. She must find her mother, and she must find out how to remove the memory block from her mind that interferes with her Sight.

Clary's eyes opening to the Sight is similar to how "the Sight" is used in the Bible, where characters often can't see certain things unless God opens their eyes and enables them to do so. For example, when Abraham banishes Hagar and Ishmael and they're wandering around in the desert without water, God opens Hagar's eyes and she sees a well.

As another example, when Abraham goes to sacrifice Isaac and the angel stops him, Abraham then sees a ram behind him and sacrifices the ram instead. God has given him eyes in the back of his head!

When Balaam goes to curse the Israelites against God's will, his way is blocked by an angel wielding a sword. He doesn't see it, but his donkey does. Eventually (after he yells at and beats his donkey for not moving onward), God opens his eyes and he sees it too.

In fact, Jewish tradition tells us that ten things were created by God at the end of the six days of creation for later use, and two of them are the ram that Abraham sacrifices and the donkey that Balaam rides.

Charlotte notes in The Infernal Devices that some mundane humans are born with a small amount of the Sight (*Clockwork Angel*, page 278). We aren't sure why some mundanes are born with the Sight, while most don't have it. Many of the household staff in the Institute have a bit of the Sight, including Sophie, Thomas, and Agatha. Traditionally, as Will explains to Tessa, servant families have the Sight, which makes sense for a paranormal household where the Sight would come in handy; and as it was in the real late 1800s in London, an Institute servant's parents probably worked at the Institute, as well.

In the real world in the sixth century BC, the Israelites were exiled in Babylon, and in an effort to preserve their culture, created hymns such as this one from the beginning of Genesis:

> *In the beginning God made heaven and earth.*
> *All was empty, chaotic and dark.*
> *And God's spirit moved over the watery deep.*
> *God said, Let light shine and it did.*
> *And God observed the light, and observed that it was good:*
> *And God separated the light from dark.*

In this fragment, the Hebrew Bible (and Christian Old Testament) describes Elohim, or God, who formed good in the world and populated the world with creatures He made in His own likeness.

Notice the emphasis on dark and light, which is abundantly evident in The Mortal Instruments and The Infernal Devices. People emerge from shadows—constantly. Indeed, people *are* shadows—constantly—before characters recognize them. The chaotic, dark aspect is represented by Lilith, by the demons, and by Valentine, Sebastian, Mortmain, and others.

The Shadowhunters and other angels represent light and good. In particular, Jace is depicted as a rising angelic creature, with his features becoming increasingly golden as the series moves forward.

Angels play important roles in both the Hebrew and Christian

Bibles, and also in many other religions. Early in Genesis (16:7–11), God's angel tells Hagar to return to Sarai and give birth to a child, who will become Ishmael. Also in Genesis, two angels in Sodom save the lives of Lot and his family. Still in Genesis, an angel intervenes when Abraham is about to kill Isaac with the knife. Note in The Mortal Instruments that the Angel Raziel tells Valentine that, while God "asked Abraham to sacrifice his own son," nobody requested this of Valentine (*City of Glass*, page 492). Only God has glory and only the Shadowhunters have a pure goal, to rid the world of demons. The reader realizes that the angel's message means that the angel views Valentine as seeking glory only for himself by falsely imprinting holy meaning into his own actions.

In The Mortal Instruments, warlock Magnus Bane helps Simon summon the Angel Raziel, which is against the rules. Magnus takes a huge risk to help Simon because even an angel's own creatures, such as Shadowhunters, aren't allowed to summon angels. This corresponds to what we see in the Bible, where people are strongly discouraged from requesting the presence of angels. The angels in The Mortal Instruments may be even more fierce than those in the Bible, for if not for Simon's mark of Cain, the Angel Raziel would probably strike him dead. Just as an angel intervenes to spare Isaac's life, Simon wants the Angel Raziel to intervene and give him the sword of the Archangel Michael so he can wrench Jonathan Herondale—Jace—from the grasp of Jonathan Christopher Morgenstern's—Sebastian's—evil.

As an aside, notice the corollary in names, Jonathan Shadowhunter, Jonathan Herondale, and Jonathan Morgenstern, leading us to guess that perhaps Jace will become the next "beginning" of the good people on Earth. Will he be, in essence, the next incarnation of Jonathan Shadowhunter?

Also notice that Jace and Sebastian are under the spell of a demonic twinning ritual that keeps them intimately bound such that the death of one means the death of the other. Good versus evil. Good Jonathan twin (Jace) versus evil Jonathan twin (Sebastian).

But back to our analysis of the Angel Raziel. He is unusual in that he won't intervene. This is interesting given how many times angels intervene in the real Hebrew and Christian Bibles. Modern people always wonder where the angels are, why they don't intervene and save us from ourselves and from all the evil and nastiness in the world. Were they around only in biblical times? Reflecting our questions and our wish that angels would come and help us sometimes, Simon points out that the Angel Raziel did indeed intervene when he brought Jace back from the dead.

In the Christian Bible (Matthew 1:20–24), an angel tells Joseph in dreams about Mary's conception by the Holy Spirit. A later passage in the New Testament tells us that at the end of time, angels will separate the evil from the good.

Angels coming to people in dreams and imparting prophecies is another parallel between the Jewish-Christian creation story and this one. For example, the Angel Ithuriel comes to Clary in dreams where she sees visions of the true demonic nature around her, helping her determine her future actions. Given that an angel told Joseph about Mary during his dreams, we figure that angels have special powers when it comes to prophecies.

So angels in The Mortal Instruments are messengers and spirits of God who come to people in dreams and also speak to people via a form of mental telepathy. As we think of them in real life, the angels in these books shine with a great goldness, stand tall, and have enormous wings. Different from our own ideas about angels, in The Mortal Instruments, Raziel creates a new race of creatures by mixing his blood with that of humans.

More than pure spirit, the angels in these books can also be starved to death, as when Valentine starves Ithuriel. And they can also die, which is quite different from how we view angels in our world. Traditional lore tells us that angels exist beyond the bounds of time and space.

The Mortal Instruments and The Infernal Devices books are filled with angel symbolism. Without the symbols, the books would fall apart. One obvious example is Tessa's clockwork angel pendant. A clear steampunk reference—the word *clockwork* nearly screams "steampunk" to science-fiction and fantasy readers—Tessa's pendant belonged to her mother, and she fingers and clutches it often.

The reader guesses that Tessa's clockwork angel pendant possesses great magical power. When Tessa Changes into dead people and channels what's left of them—possibly remnants of their souls, but souls are supposedly unbound from people when they cross into the shadow realms—her clockwork angel pendant ticks much faster. To make matters even more mysterious, Nate's dying words are to urge Tessa to wear the pendant at all times. It's so important that he begs her to swear to keep it on.

Now let's see how closely The Mortal Instruments follows the notions we've believed of angels here on Earth. In addition to the Hebrew Bible (Christian Old Testament) and the New Testament, angels are found in the Book of Mormon, the Koran, and the Dead Sea Scrolls.

Between AD 1 and 500, the Roman world was one of pagan polytheism and emperor worship. Early Christians, following the examples set by the Romans and others, often worshipped angels, with Michael being especially popular. People thought that angels were perfect beings created by God and that their bodies were made of light. This notion is carried forward in The Mortal Instruments, where even Jace is described as light and golden.

In approximately AD 500, the Syrian mystic Dionysius proclaimed in *The Celestial Hierarchy* that he was the convert "Dionysius the Areopagite," a member of the Athenian council of elders to whom Paul refers in Acts 17:34. Many people called him the Pseudo-Dionysius because of his pretentious claim. Although he was viewed by most people as a fraud, he had a huge effect on how people viewed angels.

Pseudo-Dionysius divided the angels into three classes. The first class consisted of seraphim, cherubim, and thrones; these angels were closest to God. The second consisted of dominations, principalities, and powers, who were enlightened by the first class of angels. The third consisted of virtues, archangels, and other angels, and these lowest-ranking angels were enlightened by the second class.

The Old Testament introduces the orders of seraphim and cherubim, and the New Testament introduces the orders of archangels and angels. The Judeo-Christian Bibles firmly establish the existence of nine types of angels.

In the first angelic hierarchy, we have the seraphim, cherubim, and thrones. The word *seraphim* means "having a fiery love" and "carrier of warmth," and implies the power to purify men using intense love. In The Mortal Instruments, the Shadowhunters use seraph blades made by the Iron Sisters to battle evil and protect good.

The cherubim, who represent light and the knowledge of good things, aren't in the first seven books of The Mortal Instruments and The Infernal Devices. The word *cherubim* means "the power to know and see God." Also, in The Mortal Instruments, we don't yet see the thrones, who communicate God's will to lesser angels and are patrons of peace.

The second angelic hierarchy consists of dominations, principalities, and powers. Lower in the hierarchy than thrones, the dominations also communicate God's will to lesser angels. The principalities perform executive duties related to how angels interact with humans. The powers have unshakable courage and fight Satanic evil.

The third angelic hierarchy consists of virtues, archangels, and other angels, who care for humans and their provinces. The virtues, who are extremely strong, enforce the domination's orders. The archangels watch over people, empires, provinces, and even tiny villages.

The only archangel mentioned in The Mortal Instruments series is Michael, commander of the Armies of Heaven. In the real-world Bible, angels call the Archangel Michael's name when battling evil. In Daniel 12, the prophet says that at the time the world ends, Archangel Michael will rise and protect the people.

The notion of the end of the world from the New Testament is mentioned numerous times in The Mortal Instruments series. We're told repeatedly that things are rolling toward an end, that rebirth is necessary. The biblical parallels are abundant, including characters' names such as Gabriel, Raphael, and Luke.

The Archangel Michael's sword, Glorious, is essential in Clary and Jace's battle against the demonic forces. We're told that "heavenly fire" infuses the sword and "it will burn the evil out of" an enemy (*City of Lost Souls,* page 428). This description directly ties to traditional ideas in our real world about seraphim having the power to purify men with fiery love.

Heavenly fire is definitely onstage when it shoots from the Angel Raziel's mouth straight like a "burning arrow into Valentine's chest" (*City of Glass,* page 495). And at the end of *City of Lost Souls,* fire as a holy force is everywhere. It literally "exploded" down the archangel's sword and "through Clary's arm like a bolt of electricity" (*City of Lost Souls,* page 493). Go back and read this section in the book. You'll see a lot of other references to how the angelic sword burns Jace and how his body fills with fire. This is a beautiful passage and well worth reading more than once.

Later, Cassandra Clare mentions additional biblical references to "heavenly fire" such as the "burning bush" and "the pillar of fire that went before the children of Israel," and much more (*City of Lost Souls,* page 524). In fact, this heavenly fire remains inside Jace's body, and the author describes his bones as golden, his tendons as fire, and so forth. This is another beautiful section that is well worth reading again. The entire ending of this book is magnificent, even including a reference to angel wings at the very close. This section underscores the theme about good versus evil, heavenly fire versus demonic energies. At the end of *The City of Lost Souls,* as Jace rises as a new heavenly type of being, Sebastian sends a threatening note to which he's attached angel wings taken from a live angel. That's incredibly evil, but coming from a man who condones the imprisonment and starvation of an angel, it's not surprising.

Finally, we have the angels. They are the lowest order in the hierarchy and appear throughout both the Old and New Testaments, and they include the guardian angels. We haven't seen guardian angels yet in The Mortal Instruments series.

In real-world history, in the Middle Ages between 500 and 1500, people thought that angels were created when God created the material world. Thomas Aquinas believed that angels possessed limited knowledge, bestowed upon them by God, and that they didn't have the ability to learn more. Guardian angels, those who are watchers over each human, were a popular idea during the Middle Ages.

Thomas Aquinas was one of the most influential people in Christianity. In his *Summa Theologica,* he asked and tried to answer 118 questions about angels, and he also wrote eight proofs explaining why angels exist. Aquinas wrote that God is eternal, meaning that he exists forever, totally beyond concepts such as change and time.

Between 1500 and 1648, the Reformation, people believed in the kindness of angels. Note that in The Mortal Instruments series, angels aren't necessarily kind. They're more along the lines of Old Testament God and the angels, who will strike you dead in a second if you dare do anything bad or even think something that they've taught you isn't allowed. The angel states that he would kill Simon if not for the Mark of Cain on his forehead. And don't dare to call upon an angel for a favor in The Mortal Instruments unless you come prepared for holy fire and burning death. These guys don't fool around. Summoning an angel is more dangerous than loitering around the London pier at midnight in The Infernal Devices.

In the real world, Article 12 of the Belgic Confession in 1561 stated that God created "the angels good, to be his messengers and to serve his elect," and went on to describe fallen angels, everlasting perdition, devils, evil spirits, and eternal damnation.[1] The main focus of the church during this period seemed to be on Satan, devils, and demons.

Dante's *Divine Comedy* focused strongly on Satan, hell, purgatory, and demons. And then came John Milton, who in 1667 wrote *Paradise Lost.* This classic story presents two perfect worlds, the heaven of God and the paradise of the newly created human couple. Heaven, which sparkled and was full of delight, was the place where angels worshipped God. There was nothing human in Milton's heaven, although God's heaven did provide the source for all earthly existence. Separated from this perfect heaven by "worlds and worlds" and a "vast ethereal sky" was the domain of Adam and Eve, the earthbound paradise of the newly created human couple. In The Mortal Instruments, mother-of-all-demons Lilith eventually admits that she was Adam's first wife in the Garden of Eden.

ANGEL SCHOLARS

Emanuel Swedenborg, who lived between 1688 and 1772, claimed that angels guided him while he wrote thirty books. A vision sent by God enabled Swedenborg to talk to angels, he claimed. He wasn't particularly popular with orthodox Christianity during his time, but he did contribute much lore about mysticism and angels. For example, he wrote that angels eat food, read books, get married, have sex, and breathe air.

The theologian Karl Barth, who lived between 1886 and 1968, taught that angels do not communicate with humans. Their sole communication is with God, and they serve only to dispense messages from God. How angels dispense messages without communicating with the recipients of those messages is unclear.

Geddes MacGregor, formerly Distinguished Professor of Philosophy at the University of Southern California, believes that angels are extraterrestrial beings.[2]

Peter Kreeft is professor of philosophy at Boston College. He teaches a class about angels. His book *Angels (and Demons)* attempts to explain what angels really are and what they do with their time. Kreeft believes that angelology is a science, that it uses the scientific method of gathering and explaining data. Kreeft writes that everything in the universe consists of matter except angels. He says that angels cannot die or be destroyed, that they are pure spirit, and that they are not light. They are visitors who don't belong in this universe.[3]

In the industrialized West's Jewish-Christian world from which Cassandra Clare extracts her theology, God is generally understood to be "all powerful, all knowing, and all good; who created out of nothing the universe and everything in it with the exception of Himself; who is uncreated and eternal, a noncorporeal spirit who created, loves, and can grant eternal life to humans."[4] In addition, God is usually considered male.

In The Mortal Instruments and The Infernal Devices, we have yet to see God onstage in the first seven books. We're given

WORLDVIEWS ABOUT GOD

For Hindus, God is omniscient, omnipotent, and not made of matter. The Hindus also worship other gods, but for the most part, these are perceived as manifestations of the supreme God. In the Bahá'í religion, the prophet Baha'u'llah often proclaims that God is omniscient and all perceiving. Islamic tradition gives Allah many names, such as Real Truth, the Omnipotent, the Hearer, and the Omniscient. The Buddhist Shakyamuni—a name for Buddha—was omniscient. The Tantric faith says that we should aim for omniscience ourselves, by which we will perceive cosmic consciousness, an all-knowing understanding of the universe. Zoroastrianism portrays the god Ormazd as omniscient. In Jainism, an Indian religion, monks become omniscient by meditating. Even the ancient sphinx, with its lion's body and human head, was considered omniscient.

For as long as people have believed in an omniscient God, they have questioned his existence. The German theologian Paul Tillich, who lived between 1886 and 1965, wrote,

"If you start with the question whether God does or does not exist, you can never reach Him; and if you assert that He does exist, you can reach Him even less than if you assert that He does not exist."[5] He goes on to argue that science proves no evidence for *denying* that God exists. But he also states that theologians who claim that God has spoken to them convince many people to become atheists. Why would people resist the idea of God because others claim to be prophets? Possibly it's because these people have a hard time believing that God speaks only to a few and gives them rules that everybody else must obey.

a few sprinkled clues about him but told very little about his nature or role in the entire story. As in our real world, God has various unknown names, as we're told that the "Seal of Solomon . . . contains one of the True Names of God" (*City of Glass,* page 88). As in the Old Testament, we know that God displays wrath if disobeyed, such as when he curses Lilith because she refuses to obey him or Adam in the Garden of Eden.

As with God, the devil doesn't appear onstage in the first seven novels of The Mortal Instruments and The Infernal Devices. A key plot device in the prequel series is that the clockwork creatures possess no alliance to either God or the devil. Cassandra Clare emphasizes repeatedly that the clockwork creatures are purely mechanical, not born of heaven or hell. Other than this factor, additional references to the devil are minimal, such as noting that Azazel is a "prince of Hell, second only to Lucifer" (*City of Lost Souls,* page 239). Inquisitor Imogen Herondale tells Jace that "Lucifer was rewarded for his rebellion when God cast him into the pits of hell" (*City of Ashes,* page 77), and this comment corresponds to real-world Christian belief about the devil being cast by God into hell. The reader anxiously awaits the possible onstage appearances of both God and the devil, but it's up to the author whether these two key figures will play significant roles in future books. We must wait. This reminds me of waiting to see the highest angelic authority, God, on stage in Philip Pullman's His Dark Materials. When the author finally put his God figure onstage, it was a magical moment in fiction, an absolutely brilliant creation.

No doubt about it, the theological underpinning of The Mortal Instruments series is complex. Heaven and hell are mentioned numerous times but remain vague concepts that the author may or may not develop further in subsequent novels. True epic novels leave a lot of plot strands and mysteries open as the stories unfold over the course of many thousands of pages. We glean what little we know from stray comments. For example, as mentioned earlier, Clary reminds Jace that love is "stronger than Heaven or Hell" (*City of Fallen Angels,* page 362). Another clue about the nature of heaven is that Shadowhunters believe that palaces in "Heaven" are built from adamas. Also, we're told numerous times that when two warriors are parabatai, it means that heaven knit their souls together. And there are plenty of other clues, including the key plot clue that to summon an angel requires "a blade of Heaven or Hell" (*City of Lost Souls,* page 193).

However, the reader doesn't discover the nature of either heaven or hell in any of the first seven books. Do mundane humans go to heaven and hell? Do Shadowhunters? Downworlders?

And what happens to souls at the time of death? We're told very little about this, as well. Brother Enoch comments that when Jace died, he went into a place called the shadow realms, where souls and bodies are disconnected. Is this a place of purgatory, a destination on the way to heaven or hell, or something entirely different? Nobody knows, not the readers, according to Will Herondale when he talks to Magnus Bane. And not even the Shadowhunters. And even the immortal Magnus, who has lived for an extremely long time, seeing much and acquiring great wisdom, suggests that there may be more to death than we know. He hints that there is certainly the possibility of something other than the simple cessation of life. This leaves us wondering if Shadowhunters with detached souls are resurrected, that is, born again, as Jem believes. And if so, we wonder what happens to the shell of the body that once contained the soul and now floats around in the shadow realms or in heaven/hell. It's unclear at this point in the overall story.

In a similar way, the books reference souls but provide little information as to their nature. We know that Shadowhunters, faeries, vampires, werewolves, and warlocks have souls, but demons do not have souls. The books don't define the soul for us, so I assume that it's the spark of who we are, our essence, as believed in real-world classic Christian theology. Other readers may make different assumptions as to the meaning of the soul in these novels. It's unclear at this point. We're also told that Lilith planted nightmares and burned her Mark into Jace's soul, that she now controls his soul. What this means in terms of the action of the novels is that Jace functions almost zombie-like and wooden compared to what he's like when his real soul is in complete control. Again, it's unclear to me exactly what the soul does in the context of The Mortal Instruments, though we do know that it serves as a major plot device in *City of Fallen Angels*. For Lilith to restore Sebastian's soul "in the name of the Dark" requires that Jace be present because he "was the first to be brought back, to have his soul restored . . . in the name of Light" (*City of Fallen Angels,* page 341) .

The Infernal Devices books reveal a bit about the world of ghosts, explaining that many need a lost piece of their former lives in order to actually die. These lost pieces serve as "anchors" to the real world (*Clockwork Prince,* page 4). Very little is mentioned about ghosts in The Mortal Instruments, however, just tidbits such as Isabelle once dating a ghost. The nature of these ghosts remains mysterious. Are the ghosts tied to the souls of the dead? Do the ghosts occupy the shadow realms, where souls are unbound from their bodies?

MORTAL INSTRUMENTS

CUP, SWORD, AND MIRROR

The series is called The Mortal Instruments, so clearly, these devices play a crucial role in the overall plot. The Angel Raziel gave three Mortal Instruments to the first Shadowhunters. One was the Mortal Cup, another was the Mortal Sword, and the third was the Mortal Mirror. Note the use of the word *mortal*.

An angel, supposedly immortal, supplies instruments of good to creatures who are supposedly mortal. And yet, who's really mortal and immortal in these books? We know that mundanes, or humans, are mortal, so possibly the angel gives Jonathan Shadowhunter the Mortal Instruments so he can fight for good in the mundane world. But this seems unlikely because the objective appears to be that Shadowhunters and Downworlders learn to work together to save the world from evil and darkness. We also know that mundanes can become ghosts, seeking "anchors" from their past lives before they actually die. So death—mortality—is possible, at least for mundanes. What about the other characters?

Angels traditionally might be immortal, but they may *not* be immortal in this series of books. As mentioned in my previous chapter, they can be starved to death, as when Valentine starves Ithuriel, and the author tells us outright that they can also die.

Vampires are traditionally immortal, but in this series, if a vampire's blood is drained, she dies. In addition, if Camille grants Alec's wish and removes warlock Magnus Bane's immortality, he would become mortal and eventually die. This means that vampires and warlocks are *not* necessarily immortal.

It's unknown whether faeries are immortal or just have lengthy life spans. In *City of Ashes*, we're told on page 147 that "faeries live for hundreds of years," suggesting that they do die at some point, and yet on page 202 of *City of Glass*, Valentine says that faeries are immortal.

Shadowhunters *are* mortal. They fight to the death, and Will expects to die at an early age while killing demons. So the three Mortal Instruments are probably devices for only one specific class of mortal, the Shadowhunters. Although . . .

Even the Shadowhunters may or may *not* die. Remember, when Jace died, he actually went to the shadow realms. Nobody in The Mortal Instruments series knows yet whether the shadow realms is purgatory, a destination on the way to heaven or hell, or something entirely different. And of course, Jace did come back to life.

A key plot device is that anyone possessing all three Mortal

Instruments is allowed to ask the Angel Raziel for one wish. From what the author tells us in these books, the angels don't like to be taken lightly. You can be badly burned if you try to summon one. Hence, if you summon an angel and request a wish, you'd better have an incredibly good reason. The angel need not grant your wish, so given the Angel Raziel's feelings about right and wrong, good and evil, I'd think the reason should be something along the lines of saving the entire world.

The Mortal Cup reminds me of the cups used in church that symbolically enable worshippers to drink Christ's blood. Dipped in adamas, the Mortal Cup—like the cups in churches—elevate to heavenly status only when filled with the "blood" of a heavenly creature. In this case, when an angel voluntarily lets his blood flow into the cup, it becomes the Mortal Cup.

Without the Mortal Cup, the main plot of the series wouldn't work. You could think of the Mortal Cup as the Holy Grail, which is often depicted as a cup. It must be found, and everybody's looking for it.

In fact, the Holy Grail has been associated directly with blood. Richard Wagner based his opera *Parsifal* on Wolfram von Eschenbach's poem about an Arthurian knight's quest to find the Holy Grail. In the opera, the eldest Knight of the Grail, Gurnemanz, talks about both a Holy Spear and the Holy Grail cup, which held Christ's blood as it flowed from his body on the cross. In fact, the opera also includes a Holy Spring, a body of water.

The parallels between *Parsifal* and the Mortal Instruments may or may not be intentional on the part of the author. But they do exist:

Mortal Cup = Holy Grail
Mortal Sword = Holy Spear
Mortal Mirror = Holy Spring

Fasinating, isn't it?

Just as everyone searches for the Holy Grail, Valentine searches for the Mortal Cup and steals it back when Luke and Jocelyn merge forces and try to stop him. In addition, Clary is seeking this Holy Grail of the Mortal Cup, and her search is a major plot quest in the series.

But along with the original Mortal Cup is a Second Cup, an Infernal Cup of sorts. So The Mortal Instruments has not one, but two Holy Grails, if the Holy Grail is a cup associated with blood. In an interesting twist, Sebastian gives adamas to Magdalena so she can create this Second Mortal Cup for him.

As far as I know, the myth of the Holy Grail doesn't include using blood in it to create angelic creatures or demons. But in The Mortal Instruments books, the Mortal Cup can create Shadowhunters using blood, and possibly demons as well. Clearly, it is a magical cup, for how else can you explain the notion that mixing Shadowhunter and demon blood—only in this cup— could create a new race of demonic Shadowhunters? This entire idea is central to the end of *City of Lost Souls,* the fifth book in The Mortal Instruments series. In a scene straight out of Christianity, though with a demonic twist, Lilith pours her blood into this second Mortal Cup and says, "Take of my blood and drink" (*City of Lost Souls,* page 470).

The Mortal Sword, which might correspond to the Holy Spear as portrayed in Wagner's opera, has a hilt made from adamas. Unlike the Holy Spear, this second Mortal Instrument was not used to stab the already deceased Christ when he was on the cross. In Wagner's *Parsifal,* the sorcerer Klingsor stabs the young Amfortas with the Holy Spear, and the wound doesn't heal. Legend has it that the Holy Spear is a defense weapon against the ungodly, and later, the hero, Parsifal, heals Amfortas's wound by touching it with the Holy Spear. Unlike the Holy Spear, the Mortal Sword has a magical power that forces Shadowhunters to tell the truth. As with the Mortal Cup, this is a key plot device given that Valentine wants to reverse the Mortal Sword's angelic alliance to one of demonic alliance. Also, as a clever plot maneuver, leading us down the wrong path, Brother Enoch uses the Mortal Sword in an attempt to extract the truth from Jessamine.

The final Mortal Instrument is the Mortal Mirror, which is actually Lake Lyn, otherwise known by the faeries as the Mirror of Dreams. The analogy might be to the Holy Spring in Wagner's opera. Both are bodies of water, but in the case of Wagner's opera, the water is *not* hallucinogenic. Rather, it's the source of holy water used to bless and baptize people. A major quest in The Mortal Instruments is to find the Mortal Mirror, and clues to the reader involve the many dream sequences sprinkled throughout the books. Eventually, we learn that Lake Lyn *is* hallucinogenic and triggers a wild dreamlike state in Clary. And it's at that point that we figure that Lake Lyn is probably the Mirror of Dreams. It's interesting to note that in the first Harry Potter book, *Harry Potter and the Sorcerer's Stone*, the Mirror of Erised triggers visions in Harry that he cannot ignore. He becomes addicted to these visions. This is similar to what happens with Clary and the Mortal Mirror.

The three Mortal Instruments are key: they provide the treasure quest aspect of the fantasy story. Clary must find all three Mortal Instruments to stop Valentine and Sebastian from taking over the world with evil.

7

THE CHOSEN ONES

Many novels include a main character who is the chosen one, she who will save the world and conquer evil with her goodness. The chosen one is key to the success of a quest in fantasy literature. A recent example is Katniss Everdeen in The Hunger Games. The heroine of the series, Katniss is responsible for her mother and her little sister, Prim, and then she must fight to the death, trying to thwart what is basically an evil empire. She becomes the leader of a rebellion.

In The Mortal Instruments, the chosen one is Clary Adele Fray. She binds Downworlders and Shadowhunters, and she creates new runes that help the Shadowhunters fight Valentine, Lilith, and the demonic army. She goes on treasure quests, such as when the Queen of Faeries asks her to find and return the set of faerie rings. And she's key to the main quest of the series, which is the destruction of evil by the forces of good. After all, it's Clary who convinces the crowd in the Accords Hall in Alicante to work together, and it's Clary who saves Jace and helps him find his destiny as a new angelic force.

In The Infernal Devices, the chosen one is Tessa Gray. (As an aside, does anyone else find it interesting that one character is Fray and the other is Gray?) Like Clary, she uses her special gift—in this case, channeling other characters and essentially "becoming" them—to help the Shadowhunters fight Mortmain, de Quincey, demons, automaton armies, and black magic. Like Clary, Tessa is essential to the main quest of the series, which is the destruction of evil by the forces of good.

The appeal of the hero/the chosen one might lie in his or her individuality. We all have secret dreams. Many of us aspire to create something new in the world, to shed light on an otherwise bleak society, to help people, *to find ourselves.* Pursuing our own dreams and learning who we are is all part of the uniqueness that makes every person truly human. The hero may very well be the ultimate portrayal of individuality, and hence we find her very appealing. If she can conquer demonic armies and clockwork monsters and masters of evil such as Mortmain and Valentine, then perhaps we can conquer our own fears and achieve *our* goals. Heroes give us hope.

The hero, or chosen one, in epic fantasies typically possesses special gifts. One universal gift is that the chosen one never gives up; she stands up to the worst enemies and the worst circumstances in the face of the most horrible threats and consequences. She believes in justice and doing what's right. She uses her innate gifts to do good in the world. And she often has special skills and magic abilities to help her fight her battles for the good of all mankind. This is what makes her the chosen one—because most of us can only hope to have her bravery, skill, intellect, and strength of character, and let's face it, who among us can create Portals into other dimensions, concoct magic runes out of thin air, fight demons and evil warlords, channel the dead and living into our own bodies, and so on? Heroic fantasies allow us to *dream,* for who among us wouldn't like to fulfill fantasies, ambitions, and secret wishes?

The beauty of individuality is that we can see that every one of us has something wonderful to offer, some unique talent or personality trait that can make the world a better place. A girl may be shy and possibly uncomfortable around other people, and yet she may also possess the sweetest and kindest attitude toward others—her motivations may be truly altruistic and generous. She brings beauty to the world through her acts of unselfish kindness.

Another girl may be outgoing and have lots of friends, get straight As all the time, be captain of sports teams at school, and also be a world-class musician, and yet her motivations may be selfish and narrow. She brings beauty to the world through her music.

The shy and awkward girl probably doesn't talk about her heroic tale, all the wonderful things she does for other people with no thought about getting anything in return. Think about all the people you know who fit this profile, people who help others while wanting nothing in return. These people are all heroes, aren't they? And yet their very nature prevents them from bragging to everybody about the good they do. They may not even think about it very often, but every now and then they secretly wish they could tell someone how they truly feel. For this type of person, the shared symbols of epic fantasies and a heroine in the form of the chosen one have enormous appeal. A character such as Katniss Everdeen in The Hunger Games, Clary Fray in The Mortal Instruments, or Tessa Gray in The Infernal

Devices helps us clarify our sense that we can overcome obstacles, we can achieve great things given our unique set of skills and limitations, we can fulfill our ambitions if we try hard enough, we can go on our own personal quests and in the end, succeed in becoming okay. We won't fall apart. We won't unravel due to our limitations. Our uniqueness and individuality will win against forces that erupt in our paths: nasty people, those who use us then dump us, those who hurt us, and even natural disasters that nobody controls. We, as readers, know that we'll end up okay because, after all, our heroines who are chosen ones battle much worse problems and end up okay.

It's not only children and teens who love epic fantasies and stories about chosen ones. Adult readers love Harry Potter and The Mortal Instruments, too. Adults may not always admit it, but trust me, they're intensely fascinated with heroic tales about teenagers who are chosen ones. I recently met a man who told me that he read the entire Harry Potter series, the entire Twilight series, the entire Hunger Games series, and the entire Mortal Instruments series, and he couldn't wait to read more. I should add that the guy was extremely athletic, handsome, and successful. I don't know how many people he actually tells about his reading habits, but being that I'm a writer, he probably felt comfortable discussing his love of these books with me. I've seen middle-aged men and old ladies reading Twilight, Harry Potter, The Hunger Games, and The Mortal Instruments. As the author of various companion guides to popular fantasy series, I've also received countless fan letters from both men and women, and of all ages, who love these books.

Have you ever wondered why adults are obsessed with books about heroic teens? Have you ever wondered why the appeal of the chosen one as hero is so universal, spanning all generations from little kids to the elderly? I've thought about it quite a bit over the years, and I've concluded that it's because we're all individuals with secret dreams and ambitions, and we hunger to become better versions of ourselves, to see good win over evil. We love to read about incredible adventures and goals, supernatural powers and magical abilities. It helps us emerge from our own worlds, which are often suffocating, frustrating, or dull. It helps us realize that just like these young heroes and heroines with their desire to be understood, loved, and accepted, perhaps there's hope for us, that we too will be understood, loved, and accepted.

We know that Clary has been selected by fate as the chosen one because she possesses unique talents, meaning nobody else can do what she does. For one thing, she can create runes that no other character has ever seen before, and she convinces the Shadowhunters in the Accords Hall to let her use this special talent to try to defeat the evil forces. She's as brave as Katniss Everdeen in The Hunger Games when she steps forward to assume this role. Katniss is chosen as Mockingjay, and while she doesn't want the mantle of chosen one, she finally realizes she has no option but to accept it. Clary is fated to be chosen one, as well, but in her case, it's heaven itself that compels her to do the right thing.

We know that Tessa Gray is the chosen one of The Infernal Devices from the very beginning of the prequel series. As early as page 22 of *Clockwork Angel*, the reader guesses Tessa's role when she channels Emma Bayliss for the Dark Sisters. We know that she has special powers and that somehow her clockwork angel necklace, which ticks faster when she channels Emma, is involved. The fact that her parents are unknown also adds to our realization that she's somehow unique and special. From where did she get this ability to channel the dead and living? There is no other character with Tessa's powers.

Clary has a male counterpart, a chosen hero in Jace, who's also a great romantic figure in The Mortal Instruments. He's the

Shadowhunter who has killed the most demons, and at the end of *City of Lost Souls,* Jace transforms into a golden angelic being that is unique in The Mortal Instruments universe. We guess that as the story continues to unfold, Jace will probably possess amazing gifts and powers, that he will emerge as a great force, a chosen one, to work with Clary.

I would argue that Simon is also a chosen one in these books. He's unlike all other vampires. He has special gifts, such as his ability to be in the sun and the Mark of Cain that protects him.

Would you classify any other characters as chosen ones? What do you think about Will Herondale's emerging role as a great hero? Do you think he'll possess amazing powers and supernatural gifts along the lines of Jace? Will he possess characteristics of Shadowhunters as well as automaton metal, somehow? If not, what will his special gifts be? As of this writing, with only two novels so far in the prequel series, readers have to stay tuned, but by the time you're reading *this* book, we may already know the answer.

8

BIG BAD MOTHER DEMON

LILITH, HER MINIONS, AND POSSESSION

Demons play a huge role in The Mortal Instruments series. Fallen angels, they have no souls and live in dimensional cracks. Lilith is the big bad mother of all demons—*literally*. In the world of The Mortal Instruments, she has seventeen names, among them Satrina, Ita, Kali, Batna, and Talto. You might be surprised to learn that Lilith is based on an actual demonic big bad mother in Jewish and Christian biblical legends.

Let's take a look at the similarities. First, in The Mortal Instruments, Lilith pretends to be Satrina Kendall, a band promoter, which is interesting because Cassandra Clare gives her one of the traditional names of Lilith according to real-world lore. I poked around Cassandra Clare's Tumblr page and found a post from a 1900 folklore journal, which according to Cassandra Clare quotes a "text so old no one seems to have it, called *The Mystery of the Lord*."[1] The post lists Lilith's names as "Satrina, Lilith, Abito, Amizo, Izorpo, Kokos, Odam, Ita, Podo, Eilo, Patrota, Abeko, Kea, Kali, Batna, Talto, and Partasah." Yes, Talto is one of her names, as in the Church of Talto, which I'll talk about in a minute.

But first let's look at the explanation that the fictional Lilith supplies about her origin. She claims to be the first wife of Adam; yes, the very same Adam from the Garden of Eden. According to Jewish legend, Lilith was indeed Adam's first wife. God formed both Adam and Lilith from dust, and when Adam wanted Lilith to lie beneath him, she claimed they were equal and refused to do as he wanted. Lilith and Adam argued, and Lilith flew into a rage and used God's real name in anger, which according to the Jewish religion is totally forbidden. Adam whined to God about his bad, bad wife, but even after God sent angels to talk her into submitting to Adam's desires, Lilith still refused. In The Mortal Instruments, Lilith explains that she refused to obey God and Adam, and God cursed her by killing every child she bore immediately upon birth. In real-world folklore, God does indeed curse Lilith by killing her children. In The Mortal Instruments, Lilith seeks revenge on God and all that is good by killing human babies. It's puzzling to me that God can be defined as good in this case, given that he supposedly kills all of Lilith's babies as soon as they're born because she doesn't want to be a submissive wife—it does seem a bit extreme. However, this is the case in The Mortal Instruments as well as in real-world folklore, where Lilith kills the babies of women who lie on their backs beneath men during sex.

Unlike Lilith in The Mortal Instruments, the real-world folklore Lilith is not only a baby killer, she also is the succubus who comes naked at night—her name actually means "night spirit"—and forces men to have sex with her. Another fascinating tidbit from real lore is that God made Eve from Adam's rib rather than from dust because he didn't want to saddle Adam with another difficult wife. Eve was totally submissive, except perhaps when she unleashed her inner bad girl and ate the apple. Because Lilith had already left the Garden of Eden, she wasn't around when Adam and Eve fell from grace. Hence, bad Lilith survived and good Eve died. Or so goes the real-world tale.

The Hebrew word לילית is pronounced Lilit; there is no *th* sound in Hebrew. The word may be connected to a Hebrew word *Layil* meaning "night." Isaiah 34:14 indicates that Edom will be a wasteland, and many types of demons will dwell there, including Lilit. Note that in The Mortal Instruments, Lilith "created demons by scattering drops of her blood on the earth in a place called Edom" (*City of Fallen Angels,* page 329). This passage directly corresponds to the real-world folklore tale about Lilith and Edom. It's possible Lilith is derived from the second of the three Assyrian demons known as Lilu, Lilit, and Ardat Lilit.

According to Jewish folklore, Lilith might be the third of three types of demons. The first, spirits, have no material form or body. The second, devils, appear to us as humans. The third, the lilin, appear to us as humans but also have wings.

An earlier legend from Babylonia circa 3500 BC portrays Lilith as a winged female demon. This Lilith kills human babies as soon as they are born. She's also associated with the legend of Lamashtu, who killed children, caused miscarriages, and cannibalized men. And then there's Lamia, the Libyan serpent goddess, who also killed children and seduced young men. Lilith in The Mortal Instruments is basically the demon goddess of dead children, always associated with dead babies.

By the Middle Ages, people believed that Lilith was the

devil's grandmother, the mother of all demons, and the mother of all witches and warlocks. This jibes with The Mortal Instruments, which portrays Lilith as the mother of all the half-demon warlocks, the first of all demons, and the mother of all demons. In the Jewish Kabbalah, she's so bad that she's portrayed as Samael, Satan's partner, and queen of all that is evil. It's surprising she hasn't become known as the Antichrist! But she's this bad in The Mortal Instruments, too. Remember, she tells Jace that Michael killed "the demon Sammael, whom I loved" (*City of Fallen Angels,* page 369). Clever of Cassandra Clare, I think, to sprinkle so many real-world references into her novels but with new twists. It makes the books fascinating and rich with multiple layers of meaning and depth.

Lilith as a character in The Mortal Instruments is immortal— if "killed," she enters some void of interdimensional space, from which she can return. It might take hundreds of years, but it can be done. Lilith in real-world folklore is also immortal, sort of a screeching demon-hag who howls through eternity while making people miserable. This real-world Lilith is a fairly flat character, pure evil, never learns, never evolves, never changes. And such is Lilith in The Mortal Instruments: pure evil, never learns, never evolves, never changes. She has reasons for what she does—vengeance against God and Adam—but after existing since the dawn of time, you'd think this creature might have a little heart already.

Lilith and all the minion demons beneath her are crucial to the plot of The Mortal Instruments series. In the overall war between good and evil, we have Shadowhunters versus demons. If we took the demons out of the mix, we'd have to replace them with something else equally as horrific—possibly clockwork armies?

We know from the first few chapters of *City of Bones* that

demons are going to be central to this epic story. Very quickly, Clary encounters and kills her first demon.

The same is true of the prequel series, The Infernal Devices. Immediately, we know that demons will play a big part. Right away, Will Herondale and Jem are fighting a demon.

What do we know about demons in these books? Well, we know they have no souls because the Angel Raziel explicitly tells us this. We're also told that "their consciousness comes from a sort of energy" (*Clockwork Angel,* page 85). In our real-world folklore, demons were considered spiritual beings who sometimes took corporeal form. The word *spiritual* in this context refers to a conscious form of energy, a very similar idea to that in The Mortal Instruments. In medieval times, theologians thought that demons inhabited the dark and stormy parts of the atmosphere, which corresponds to the interdimensional realms inhabited by demons in The Mortal Instruments. By living in the atmosphere, demons could erupt at any time and impose their evil will upon humans.

Because the demons run on this strange energy, apparently devices in the novels can detect the energy and, hence, the presence of demons. Think about it: What if demons really did exist? They'd have to be powered by some sort of energy, and if so, a device could conceivably be created to detect the energy. Once you accept the idea of demons, anything goes. Created by Henry in the late 1800s in The Infernal Devices and used constantly in modern times in The Mortal Instruments, the Sensor—this demon device—must somehow tune in to whatever wavelength the demonic frequency is transmitting. How this is done, we don't know, but it's an interesting idea. I'm not sure how such a device would work in modern times, much less in the late 1800s, but it is fun to read the scenes in which Henry's early prototypes misfire and cause problems.

In our real-world folklore, although demons don't literally exist in hell, they are in constant contact with the fires of hell. Some theologians also believe that demons spent time in Earth's atmosphere, then went to hell and tormented people while other demons took their place in Earth's atmosphere. Back and forth these demons went between Earth and hell.

But there's much more about them in these novels. *So much.* We have demon languages, demon summonings, demon babies, demon smells, demon entrapment in pentagrams, female demon cults, demon towers, demon fire, demon poison, demon venom, demon magic, demon energy, demon diseases, demon metal, demon blood, and even demon humor.

Before delving into these subjects—not to mention possession, twinning rituals, and angel-demon mixed-blood baby experiments—see if you can guess which of the many dozens of Mortal Instruments demons are based on real-world folklore demons. This is tough, unless, of course, you happen to be a seminary student or a minister. If you're an ordinary person (like me), you may have to consult a demonic encyclopedia or two. If you don't happen to have one sitting on your nightstand, then go ahead and cruise the Internet, seeking information about Moloch and Kuri demons, Elapid and Vetis demons, and so forth. I scoured some demon encyclopedias and learned a bit about some common demons, which I share with you below.

Eidolon demons are shape-changers in The Mortal Instruments. Mrs. Dark is actually an Eidolon demon, which is why she knows how to teach Tessa to shape-change. Is there such a thing as a shape-changing Eidolon demon? Well, the ancient Greeks called ghostly images of dead and living people Eidolons, but phantomlike images aren't exactly *shape-changing demons.* Examples of shape-changing demons do exist in mythology, such as the Buddhist and Hindu Rakshasas, which not only shape-change but also do all sorts of evil things, such as eating human flesh. In ancient stories, they can also disappear at will and fly. The shape-shifting snakelike Nagas are sometimes depicted as wicked and other times as protectors, as in the case of Mucalinda, the Naga that protects Buddha.

Then we have Greater Demon Abbadon, who claims to control the "wind and the howling darkness" (*City of Bones,* page 353). Go back to *City of Bones* and read the description of the Abbadon on page 352. Do you think this demon exists in real-world mythology?

Most stories about Abbadon consider it a place of death and destruction rather than a demon. However, in the New Testament's Revelation 9:11, Abaddon is mentioned as the name of a creature who is "a king, . . . the angel of the bottomless pit." He is the destroyer of things on Earth, and in fact, the Hebrew word "Ibaddon" means "utter destruction."

Dragon demons are mentioned but haven't really come onstage yet in the books. Perhaps we don't yet have a dragon demon character because they're almost extinct. I don't have to point out to you that dragons are prevalent in mythology and many fantasy series.

Moloch demons are minor characters in The Mortal Instruments, but in real mythology—and in Leviticus 18—they were evil gods to whom people sacrificed their children.

Azazel is a powerful demon, not only in The Mortal Instruments, but also in Leviticus of the Bible, where he's central to Yom Kippur, the day of atonement. On this high holy day, the priest chooses a pair of twin goats, similar to how Azazel is confronted with the problem of Jace and Sebastian, who are joined by Lilith's twinning ritual. The priest uses a simple lottery system to select one goat to sacrifice and one goat to be sent away. In The Mortal Instruments, Azazel selects Sebastian to slide into hell, thus freeing Jace from his "twin." After sacrificing the first goat, the priest in Leviticus places his hands on the second goat and symbolically dumps the sins of all the people on the animal. He then sends the goat—the original scapegoat, by the way—into the desert, where it is pushed off a cliff and sent to Azazel and death. In this way, the separating of the twin goats, the people atone for their sins. Because Jace rises as an angelic presence of hope at the end of *City of Lost Souls,* he too is separated from his "twin" and will help the people with their quest for good in the world.

There are many more types of demons: Oni, Belial, Iblis, Behemoth, Croucher, Hydra, Vetis, Elapid, Dahak, Shax, Marax, Yanluo, and Thammuz, not to mention the demon hordes that come in all shapes and sizes.

The Belial demon, also called Beliar, is defined as unholy and worthless. In 2 Samuel 16:7 of the Bible, an enemy named Shimi ben Gera stones King David, curses at him, and calls him by the name Belial: "Come out, thou bloody man, and thou man of Belial" (King James Version). King David pities Shimi and promises that Shimi will not be killed as long as David is alive. But as he's dying, David tells his son Solomon to take Shimi down to Sheol, which means the underworld, the place of death. There were no promises about what would happen to Shimi after David's death, and so Solomon kills him. In Psalm 18:5, the phrase *nachalei belial* means "floods of ungodly men," and translated by the Catholic Bible, "streams of the devil."

The Iblis demon in the Koran is actually an Arabic rendering of *diabolos* in Greek. We all know what diabolos means, right? *The devil.*

The Hebrew word *behema* means "animal," and a *behemoth* is a giant oxlike beast in Job 40. A behemoth demon fits with this description, oddly enough, because in some interpretations, this oxlike beast is actually a precursor of the Apocalypse. Indeed, in the Middle Ages, Christians associated the behemoth with Satan.

IN WITH FORTUNE, OUT WITH THE ONI!

The Oni demon comes from Japanese folklore and legends. He moves between the worlds of the living and dead, and while he isn't inherently as evil as, say, a demon who eats children, the Oni causes trouble anyway.

In addition to the supernatural Oni demon, there's a slight variation. Throughout Asia, myths told of storm spirits that created natural disasters, and these spirits were known as Oni. This type of Oni demon hurls fierce winds and drums thunder across the skies. The Japanese would perform ceremonies to attempt to expel the Oni demons on the last day of each year. Chanting, "In with fortune, out with the Oni!" people scattered beans in all directions, hoping to banish evil in the form of natural disasters.

The Oni's appearance differs from tale to tale. In some cases, the demon has horns; in others, he has one large staghorn. He typically has fangs and claws, and he looks worried with a furrowed brow. I've seen Japanese Oni clay figures, and they remind me of the large gargoyle sitting by my front door. So if you know what a typical gargoyle looks like, then you know what an Oni looks like.

The Buddhist Oni are a bit different in that they don't always represent forces of evil. For example, an Oni might be a former—but now deceased—clergyman whose spirit protects his former followers from natural disasters. One such Oni was Tendai priest Gazan Ryogen, whose soul stayed on Mt. Hiei, where he had restored temple buildings.

Do you remember Yanluo, who murdered Jem's parents? This Greater Demon was the one who got Jem hooked on the demon poison in Shanghai. This provides a major plot device in The Infernal Devices because Jem is slowly dying from his addiction, which makes him a tragic character. It colors his entire personality, and kind people (such as Tessa) can't bear to hurt him. Will is tormented by Jem's addiction, and he too is a tragic figure; in a sense, you can almost think of Will as dying slowly, too, as he drains away in sadness and despair.

But what about the demon himself, Yanluo? Is he real in our mythology, or did Cassandra Clare totally make him up? Can you guess?

Could he be Yao, the mythical Chinese emperor who helped vanquish horrible winds? Probably not, because Yao was a figure of good.

Could he be Yaoshi-fo, the Chinese physician Buddha, who devotes himself to curing people of both physical and mental illness? Probably not. He's a figure of good, too.

How about Yama, Yaksas, or Yamantaka?

(I'm trying very hard to tease you into guessing the obvious answer.)

As if you haven't figured this out by now, Yanluo *is* an actual figure in real-world mythology. Like Yanluo in *Clockwork Angel* and *Clockwork Prince,* the real-world Yanluo is a Chinese figure, but unlike Jem's demon, he judges the dead. Also known as Yan Wang, he is the god of the dead, the prince of the underworld. He corresponds to Yama, the Buddhist ruler of all the dead. As prince of hell, he draws souls from corpses using a noose, and he rides a black buffalo. As a side note, the Japanese call this same figure Emma-ten or Emma-O, king of hell.

Although The Infernal Devices prequel series uses clockwork automatons rather than demonic armies, the plan is to infuse and animate the automatons with demonic energies. Because this is a prequel—it happens before the time of The Mortal Instruments—the reader wonders how Cassandra Clare will shift from demonic energy-infused mechanical devices to actual demonic creatures. In the time of The Mortal Instruments, have the clockwork armies been destroyed? And is there no memory of them and how horrible they were? With technology much more advanced, why hasn't some evil person in modern times created another clockwork army with even more power? I also wonder if Sensors that pick up demonic frequencies will work on clockwork armies infused with demonic energies. It's hard to wait for the sequel, but I have no choice!

In a nice twist on vampires and werewolves, Cassandra Clare tells us that both can be created by demon diseases. Kyle explains that the demon disease causing lycanthropy makes werewolves more prone to modern problems such as suicide and domestic violence. Other novels suggest that werewolves and vampires are caused by plagues and diseases, but demon diseases with resulting suicide and domestic violence rates are clever.

The last thing I want to talk about in this chapter is possession. What does this mean in our real world, and what does it mean in The Mortal Instruments? Is Jace actually possessed?

First we must note that, for a long time, Jace believes he's a monster because he thinks he's part demon. This is a huge motivation for how Jace handles his love for Clary. He mistakenly thinks she's his sister, and since he's madly in love with her, well, he must be a monster. Forbidden love is a wonderful romantic plot mechanism, and in this case, it works really well. Brother and sister should not be in love. And yet, how can Jace truly be a demon-monster if he *is* in love? Because remember, demons have no souls, and hence they cannot love. Clary finally puzzles through all of this and explains it to Jace.

But whether he's part demon or part monster, is he actually possessed by a demonic spirit? He has terrible nightmares about killing her, and instead of telling her about the nightmares, he does what most people do. He avoids telling her the truth and, indeed, he avoids her altogether. Again, it's Clary who provides the voice of reason, at least in the context of demonic influence, that is. Is it possible to love somebody as much as Jace loves Clary and yet have nightmares about killing her? Is he correct in thinking he must be part demon, or is it instead possible that he is . . .

possessed?

Clary figures out that the nightmares are planted in his head, which I think is another way of saying he's possessed.

In a wonderfully complex scenario, we learn that when Jace died, he lost the ritual protections he had as a Shadowhunter against demonic "influence," or what I term possession. But of course, Jace was resurrected—he had to return to the story because he's a central character—at which time, Lilith could step in and start planting those nightmares. The novel insists that it isn't possession but rather "influence" (*City of Fallen Angels*, page 271). I don't quite see the difference. Lilith controls him, right down to his soul, where her Mark has burned deeply in. In essence, Clary must perform an exorcism to rid Jace of Lilith's Mark, though it isn't described as such. But again, isn't this just another form of exorcism, when Clary rids Jace of Lilith's control over his mind, heart, and soul?

In *City of Lost Souls*, Lilith performs a weird "twinning ritual," in which she binds Jace to Sebastian. In an effort to describe how the twinning ritual differs from actual possession, we learn that "in a possession there is often some part of the person's original consciousness left intact. Those who have been possessed speak of watching their own actions from the outside, crying out but unable to be heard" (*City of Lost Souls*, page 118). Just as it seems a fine hair to split between Lilith's control of Jace's soul as "influence" rather than possession, it seems here that Jace is possessed by Sebastian. Certainly, the definition of *possession* in *City of Lost Souls* seems to correspond to what happens to Jace when he bears Lilith's Mark. Back then, he still knew he was inside himself because he caused a temporary removal of the Mark's properties so he could express romantic feelings for Clary.

In an incredible book that I feel compelled to quote—it is called *Demon Possession and Allied Themes: Being an Inductive Study of Phenomena of Our Own Times* and was published not in our own times but in 1894—Reverend John L. Nevius describes his experiences with demonic possession in China, Japan, India, and various Western countries.

He identifies and defines four distinct stages of possession.[2] First, he says, the demon "influences" the victim in a "tentative" manner. He explains that "in this stage cases are often unpronounced in their character, leaving it difficult to determine whether they are to be classed with demon-possession, idiocy, lunacy, or epilepsy." So according to this definition, Jace is not under the "influence" of Lilith, is he? She hasn't been tentative in her approach to him. Rather, she put her Mark over his heart. Nor does he appear to be an idiot or a lunatic, or to have epilepsy!

In stage two, the victim struggles against the demon, but eventually he falls beneath the demon's spell. "This may be called the transition stage or the crisis," writes Reverend Nevius. "It is comparatively of short duration." It's safe to assume that Jace already passed through stage two. He already has Lilith's Mark on him, he's not "influenced" as in stage one, nor is he transitioning to demonic possession, certainly not as defined by Nevius.

In the third stage of possession, the demon trains the victim to do as the demon wants. The victim seems fairly normal and healthy, and he continues to develop into an evil entity as demanded by the demon. Jace doesn't seem normal and healthy while under Lilith's spell. Nor does he seem normal and healthy while under Sebastian's spell. In the first case, he's like a zombie-tormented Jace, and in the second case, he simply functions as a zombie clone of Sebastian.

In the full-blown fourth stage of possession, the victim is the demon's slave. The demon controls the victim: what he thinks (Jace's nightmares) and what he does (actions defined by Sebastian).

Luckily for Jace, he's saved not once but twice from this possession—oh, okay, you can call it influence, if you must. And having the mother of all demons cut from him, as well as Sebastian, Jace emerges as what might come to be the father of all angels. For who knows what will happen in subsequent books, as Jace now fulfills his fate as an angelic wonder of some kind?

INFERNAL DEVICES

AUTOMATON MONSTERS?

Automatons aka clockwork creatures serve as demonic entities in The Infernal Devices. Demons exist, of course, but the heroes also must overcome the infernal devices, possibly the automaton monsters. I say "possibly" because, as I explain later in this chapter, the infernal devices may actually be the evil counterparts of the three Mortal Instruments. Mortmain's plan in The Infernal Devices is to create an evil clockwork army just as Valentine's plan in The Mortal Instruments is to create an evil demonic army. Regardless, the automaton monsters are indeed infernal devices, so we'll consider them as such.

An automaton is a machine that operates independently.

That's the simple definition. Some people attribute intelligence to automata, but a machine with artificial intelligence would be a form of robot or android. If you strip out intelligence, the notion of a soul, and the need for a human to control the machine, then at its core, it is defined as an automaton.

Steampunk, which I'll discuss in a later chapter, is a subgenre of science fiction in which automata are central to the story. The Infernal Devices series clearly falls within the realm of steampunk and uses some of its key tropes, such as clockworks. Indeed, the titles of the books incorporate the word *clockwork*.

In the sixteenth century, German clockmakers made novelty clocks in which animated figures moved to entertain viewers. These might be considered the precursors to what we think of as steampunk automata. Then in the eighteenth century, still before the time of The Infernal Devices, the Jaquet-Droz family in Geneva commissioned the creation of more complicated mechanical figures that moved to music.

Clockwork Angel opens in April 1878. This was on the cusp of the golden age of automata, which spanned approximately 1880 through 1920. A leading manufacturer of automata was Roullet & Decamps in Paris, founded by Jean Roullet, run later by Ernest Decamps—Roullet's son-in-law—and then by Gaston Decamps, who was Ernest's son. Roullet & Decamps were known for their extremely complex automata that included fancy components such as gorgeous French costumes, dolls' heads from both France and Germany, and Swiss musical mechanics. During the golden age of automata, the Blaise Bontems company in Paris made singing birds automata.

In The Infernal Devices, we have Mortmain and Company, a huge manufacturer of machine tools during the time when, in the real world, clockwork devices were all the rage. Axel Mortmain, evil overlord of automata, seeks revenge for what he

CIGAR-SMOKING AUTOMATA

Other leading manufacturers of real-world automata during the time period of The Infernal Devices included Vichy, which made clown automata and even "man in the moon" automata with unusually expressive faces. Leopold Lambert's company made mechanical figures that performed simple actions, but what set Lambert apart was that his figures had heads and costumes made by some of the finest doll companies in the world. Lambert, who had worked for the Vichy company and was a master automata designer, sold mechanical figures that blew bubbles and even smoked cigars. I can imagine one of Mortmain's automata standing on a street corner—in the shadows, of course—blowing smoke rings. That would be highly amusing, wouldn't it?

Of all the makers of automata, one of the most sophisticated was founded by Jean-Marie Phalibois in Paris, whose designs were extremely complex. Phalibois used ivory, mother-of-pearl, and brass, and his automata performed in groups and included such oddities as monkey figures dressed as people.

views as the wrongful death of his parents, John Thaddeus and Anne Evelyn Shade. The key difference, of course, between Axel Mortmain and real-world clockmakers such as Roullet & Decamps and Blaise Bontems is that Mortmain is evil and wants to infuse his automata with demonic energies. I doubt that the Parisian makers of automata ever entertained that notion at all.

When de Quincey created the automatons, the figures were much as in our real world and had to be wound up like clocks before they could run independently. They were mechanisms, not alive, not with souls, not with intelligence of their own. The clockwork army consists mostly of human-shaped automatons that remind me of Frankenstein's monster. They have jerky movements and "smooth ovals of metal patched here and there with uneven bits of human skin" (*Clockwork Angel,* page 394). But the fictional automata of The Infernal Devices are more bizarre than even Frankenstein's monster. Sure, they're created with bits and pieces of real human hearts and skin, and sure, the Dark Sisters are robbing graves and harvesting everything from organs to bones to hair. However, these automata have the potential to become a crazed robotic army hell-bent on death and destruction. If the black magic binding charm is generated during the full moon, then presto, an evil spell will give life to these clockwork monsters.

And let's consider Miranda, whose chest is sliced open to reveal copper and brass devices and tubing. She even has a metal tongue. According to Henry, she's based on designs by Leonardo da Vinci, drawings in which mechanical creatures sit, walk, and turn their heads.

How real is Henry's explanation about Leonardo da Vinci? *Very real.*

In Italy in 1495, Leonardo da Vinci designed—and may have constructed—the first humanoid automaton. Much as Henry claims, Leonardo designed his robot knight to sit, wave its arms, and turn its head. The automaton was designed to open and close its "mouth" much as Miranda might open and close her mouth. The definitive sketches—or blueprints, as they might be known in The Infernal Devices—are in Leonardo's *Book of Mechanics.*

Leonardo da Vinci had studied extremely early attempts at developing mechanical devices, including ancient Greek texts. For example, Archita of Taranto in the fourth century BC created a dove from wood using mechanisms so the dove could fly. Archita carefully devised his dove with perfectly balanced weights and internal air currents. In 1515, Leonardo attempted something very similar when he created animals from wax and filled them with air currents, then blew into the shapes so they temporarily flew.

Other ancient texts that are little known today include *Pneumatics* by Philon of Byzantium, from as far back as the second century BC. It's amazing to think that people more than two thousand years ago knew about pneumatics, another steampunk staple. Remember, machines have been around for an extremely long time, and coupling mechanical knowledge with Leonardo's genius-level grasp of the body would very well lead someone of his intelligence to conceive of humanlike automata. Indeed, Leonardo's private library included a reference to *Libro di Filone De Acque,* which scholars believe must refer to Philon's *Pneumatics.*

In approximately 1508, Leonardo created an automaton bird that "flew" along a cable by means of a double-crank mechanism. The bird flapped its wings, and during the real-world time of The Infernal Devices, birds such as these were sold as toys.

He also created his own highly elaborate and detailed drawings of human joints and how they operate. These drawings are incredibly famous as templates for his paintings of the human body.

Combining his knowledge of both the human body and mechanics, Leonardo devised ways to control and move his automata. In 1478, he created an automaton that may very well have been the precursor to modern robots. It was a lion that "walked" across the room in front of King Francis I of France. It was a truly mechanical beast complete with programmable cart, wheels, cables, cranks, gears, and so forth.

In terms of automaton sophistication, by the 1600s, Kircher had described how to build a mechanical organ, Blaise Pascal in 1642 had invented his mechanical adding-and-subtracting calculator, and Gottfried Wilhelm Leibniz in 1672 had designed a calculator that not only added and subtracted but also multiplied, divided, and found square roots. As a sidenote, I find it interesting that Pascal, who is considered a major figure in the history of computer science, sold only about fifty of his calculators in 1642.

In the 1700s, French inventor Jacques de Vaucanson created angel automata, as well as a four-hundred-part mechanical duck in the 1730s that appeared to eat corn and swim—and defecate!

In the 1770s, Pierre Jaquet-Droz created an android with a self-contained writing mechanism, and Henri Maillardet sold androids that not only wrote but also told fortunes. By 1796, Hosokawa Yorinao in Japan published a three-volume manual called *Sketches of Automata*.

Punch-card programming for mechanical weaving looms existed in 1805, and then circa 1825–1839, Charles Babbage designed his Difference Engine followed by his Analytical Engine, which he designed with Ada Lovelace. Neither machine was completed, but both provided a distinct framework for today's steampunk movement.

In 1868, Zadoc P. Dederick and Isaac Grass obtained their patent for a "steam man," a mechanical man that would pull a steam-driven cart. This was ten years before the opening of the period during which *Clockwork Angel* takes places.

By 1877, a mere one year before *Clockwork Angel* opens, Lord Kelvin was able to demonstrate that mathematical problems can be solved by machines. And then it was in 1893 that George Moore built the first walking "steam man."

In The Infernal Devices, the automata can obey human commands, something real-world automata didn't do in the 1880s. Tessa is able to shape-change into Nate, then command a killer automaton to grab the real Nate. The automaton obeys the command of what it "perceives" to be Nate, who is actually Tessa, of course.

Automata in our real world were based in large part on earlier clockwork mechanisms. This fact draws an obvious parallel between the clockwork creatures, the automata, and Tessa's clockwork pendant, which possesses some magical power we don't yet know about (as of the end of *Clockwork Prince*—I'm writing this chapter in December 2012, several months before *Clockwork Princess* is released). We do know that the clockwork pendant protects her from the automata, which withdraw from it. In this way, it works much as Simon's Mark of Cain, which repels vampires such as Raphael as well as demons and even angels as powerful as Raziel.

Real automata used mechanical elements in which the movement of one triggered the movement of additional elements. By winding up an automaton, it performs the same motions repeatedly until it winds back down. In this way, it resembles clockwork because it runs in a cyclical way.

The early humanlike automata incorporated very primitive programming to do things such as write and play musical instruments. Their movements were based on mechanical "cam" versions of what is now known as read-only memory (ROM). The cams were discs that rotated on cylinders, and rods attached the cams and the various parts, such as feet for walking. This is why in The Infernal Devices, the automata stumble forward like Frankenstein's monster, as I mentioned earlier.

Yet without Sensors, how do these automata stumble correctly in the direction of someone like Tessa? How do they attack? How do they inspire true fear? While their mechanisms operate cyclically, while they perform the same patterns over and over again, they do so without any conscious knowledge or any remarkable direction. The real automata may have appeared to dance or write, but these actions were predicated on patterns. A twirling automaton wouldn't suddenly leap off the dance floor, grab a man's arm, and then break into an elaborate tango with him—all on the spur of the moment.

Is it possible that once the automaton monsters are infused

with demonic energies, they will have souls or real intelligence? We know that demons do *not* have souls, though they do have independent intelligence—that is, they have their own minds. So perhaps the clockwork monsters won't have souls, either, but will possess some rudimentary internal intelligence. Here, I'm speculating, because like everyone else, I must wait for further books in the series to find out what Cassandra Clare has in mind.

If an automaton suddenly has demonic energies, will it still be a machine, or will it now be a living creature? If a living Shadowhunter is implanted with demon metal, if he is infused with a weird sort of energy from this metal, will he be part machine and part Shadowhunter? This type of creature will retain his soul, won't he? But just what is a soul?

French philosopher René Descartes famously wrote, "I think, therefore I am." What he meant was that a person considers herself as a distinct individual, a self with a soul. Plato thought that the gods inserted souls into people. He considered souls to be of a nature not yet understood—possibly a weird form of energy? Aristotle believed that the soul is a "form" taken by a person and does what is necessary to keep the person alive. He also thought that different types of animals have different types of souls, that the human soul incorporates reason and conscious knowledge of the self.

According to the Old Testament, the soul is life. When the human dies, the soul dies. In the New Testament, the soul is immortal, and depending on the human's actions during his life, his soul will either remain in eternal bliss or eternal hell. During the time of the early church, people believed that the Old Testament soul was in the heart and liver. They also believed that the New Testament soul was invisible and existed everywhere— as well as nowhere—at all times. Yet even existing within these odd parameters, the soul also had special abilities inside the person's skull.

I've assumed that the "infernal devices" are the actual clockwork creatures. Perhaps the infernal devices will be like the Mortal Instruments in that they are somehow used to create a new race of demonic half-mechanical, half-biological magical creatures. Jem says something in *Clockwork Prince* that baffles me. On page 358, he calls Henry's device an "infernal device." I wonder why this is called an "infernal device," given that it jams the mechanism the clockwork creatures, whom I consider to be infernal devices.

Another puzzling bit of information about the infernal devices comes from *City of Lost Souls.* When Sebastian calls forth Lilith and she gashes her wrist, letting her blood drop into the Mortal Cup, she then calls it the Infernal Cup. This suggests that the infernal devices will be like the Mortal Instruments. So perhaps the clockwork creatures aren't the infernal devices, after all.

I can tell you this: I'm *extremely* eager to read the next book in this series. I'm not sure if I like Clary and Jace's story better than Tessa and Will's story, but I do know that I'm fascinated by the clockwork creatures and want to see what the author does with them.

10

AND WHAT ABOUT THOSE BAD GIRLS?

gave you a bad boys chapter, so it's ony fair to provide a bad girls chapter. Who's the most evil, the most despicable, and why? Is it Mrs. Dark or Mrs. Black, the Faerie Queen of the Seelie Court, Camille Belcourt, or perhaps Lilith, the mother of all demons? Readers decide: Who's the worst of them all? In today's world, would they be considered "mean girls"?

This fun little section looks at a few of the worst cases of bad girls in The Mortal Instruments and The Infernal Devices. See if you agree with my assessments!

On a scale of 1 to 10, with 1 being nice and 10 being absolutely evil, I give Camille Belcourt an 8. Ordinarily, I'd probably give her a 9, but I like her character too much to do that. Why do

I rate her as an 8 on my evil scale? Because as with the bad boys, anyone who kills people is rotten. And Camille admits to killing Shadowhunters. Maryse Lightwood tells her that the sentence for her crime is death, just as it might be in our real world. It doesn't matter if she kills while under orders from a creature more powerful than she is; it only shows her to be a coward—doesn't it? If you were told to kill a bunch of people by a bully who threatens you with extermination, what would you do? Probably not kill the people, unless your morals are slipping.

On a scale of 1 to 10, I give Elaine Lewis a 2. She's nice at heart. She's just a little crazy when it comes to religious symbolism and hocus-pocus fears. When she locks Simon out of the house because she's afraid of his strange new attributes—he's a vampire!—she acts out of fear, not because she's evil. It hurts him, so I can't give her a pure 1 on the nice-to-evil scale. The entire section is highly amusing, by the way, in which she plasters the front door with the Star of David, the Chai, Tefillin, a Mezuzah, and even a Hamesh (Hamsa), Hand of God. Traditionally, Jewish people don't use these items to ward off evil. Certain mystic followers, say, those who are heavy into the Kaballah, may believe in icons, symbols, and numerology. Unlike the Christian cross, however, Jews don't use the Star of David to ward off vampires. The Chai is a symbol meaning "living" and is not used to ward off vampires. The Tefillin? Orthodox and very Conservative Jewish men wear Tefillin on their foreheads and arms closest to their heart when praying to God during weekday mornings. These are boxes containing portions of the Torah, and men attach them with long, thin straps to keep God close to their minds and hearts while praying. They aren't really used to ward off evil. The Mezuzah is on the doorframe of Jewish homes and also contains inscribed parchment; in this case, Hebrew verses beginning with the Shema prayer. Like the Tefillin, the Mezuzah is a reminder of God's presence and blessings. It's not really a device to ward off evil. The Hamesh is an unusual Jewish symbol in that it might mean the Hand of God, but on the other hand, it might refer to the multi-cultural hand-and-eye symbol that protects against the evil eye. I love Cassandra Clare's use of these traditional Jewish symbols as ways to keep evil spirits out of the Lewis household. We so often read about vampires and Christian symbols that it's fun to read a book or two in which symbols from other religions are used. Given the use of garlic with the Christian cross to ward off vampires, I was waiting for the author to throw in a matzo ball or two!

What do you think about Maureen, the fairly minor charac-ter who rises to the leader of the vampire clan after killing Ca-mille? Do you think Maureen is evil because she kills Camille, and if so, do you rate her a 9 or 10 on my scale? Because she's a relatively minor character, I'll stick her with an 8.

For me, the obvious choice for most evil female character is Lilith. She even eclipses Mrs. Dark and Mrs. Black. Lilith kills babies. Not good. In fact, extremely evil. Like Valentine, her rat-ing flies off the scale. She too gets a rating of 10 raised to the ten-millionth power.

Is it evil to do a favor when you're getting something in re-turn? When the Faerie Queen of the Seelie Court, who is de-scribed as "cool" and "menacing" and "calculating (*City of Ashes,* pages 170–171), tells Clary she can be freed with a kiss, she has an angle. Remember, faeries don't help humans without having something up their sleeves. She's probably a 4 on my scale. What do you think?

Now then . . . the Dark Sisters. They rate a 10+, for sure. If you kidnap somebody and torture him for a long time, you're evil. If you harvest body parts in hopes of someday orchestrat-ing an evil army to bring chaos and demonic hell upon the world, then you're evil.

In addition, both Dark Sisters extort money from mundanes via the Pandemonium Club—and by the way, don't you love how Cassandra Clare embedded the word "demon" into the name of the club? When mundanes fall into debt due to the magical games at the club, the Dark Sisters impose terrible rates on what they owe to bail them out.

Did you have trouble keeping track of which Dark Sister was Mrs. Dark and which one was Mrs. Black? Or did they feel interchangeable to you? Which one did you hate the most?

Have you also wondered why both of the Dark Sisters use the married prefix "Mrs."? Who would be stupid enough to want to marry these creatures? I can only pity Mr. Dark and Mr. Black.

So which bad girl is the most evil and despicable of them all? What do you think? While I have to go with Lilith, who after all is the mother of all demons, Mrs. Dark and Mrs. Black are a very close second. All three of these characters are pure evil without even a glimmer of sweetness in them.

In today's world, which ones would be considered "mean girls"? This is different from being the most evil of them all. Mean girls aren't necessarily pure evil like Darth Vader. They're catty, selfish, and mean-spirited. They gossip, they spread false rumors, they attack peoples' characters on a whim, just to amuse themselves. They like to make people squirm and suffer. It helps them feel good about themselves. But inside, they might actually be sad, unsure about themselves. They might actually lack self-confidence because it takes more guts to stand up for what's right than to attack other people. So they're not necessarily pure evil.

So who is *your* choice for mean girl of The Mortal Instruments and The Infernal Devices? If I have to choose one, I must go with Jessamine Lovelace. While Isabelle Lightwood is something of a mean girl for a long time in The Mortal Instruments, she evolves into a fun character. Jessamine is very sympathetic, as well—tragic and sad, and I can't help but feel sorry for both of these characters. However, Isabelle seems the stronger of the two and, despite her initial arrogance and nasty comments, she's on the side of good and a fierce defender of her friends. Jessamine is the weaker of the two, falling for Nate and betraying Tessa.

Finally, which of the bad girls is your favorite, for any reason whatsoever? I'm rather fond of Camille Belcourt. She's sophisticated and glamorous, evil yet with an undercurrent of sadness and kindness, which may be hidden beneath her vampire queen veneer, but I believe there's good in her deep on the inside.

11

STEAMPUNKING YOU

The books in The Infernal Devices are steampunk novels. This is clear from the prologue of the first book in the series, which opens in London in April 1878, with steamships, clockwork angels, gas lamps, and squalid city conditions. In fact, the titles of the novels give it away: we're in steampunkland. This chapter describes steampunk as a genre, the tropes, the popularity, the fan movement, and ties these ideas and facts to The Infernal Devices.

Some people call steampunk "the new Gothic literature." It's retro cool with a Jules Verne and H. G. Wells techie feel, yet it's also futuristic with a William Gibson cyberpunk feel. The technology is Victorian and relies on pneumatics and steam power with lots of copper, brass, and wood.

In the science-fiction and fantasy community, steampunk has grown into a full-blown subgenre with its own conventions and fleet of novels. Its fashion is Victorian and Edwardian, and its technology fuses Gothic horror with futuristic science. It's perfect for a romantic fantasy epic such as The Infernal Devices because of its Victorian-Gothic nature, the frock coats and top hats, the long dresses, the horse-drawn carriages, the foggy streets lit only by gas lamps. Steampunk recaptures the thrill of Jules Verne and H. G. Wells novels with its alternate universes and dimensions, steamships and steam-powered automata, and it places these retrofuturistic thrills squarely within the Industrial Revolution's squalor and grime.

The Infernal Devices is a wonderful fusion of steampunk and dark paranormal romantic fantasy. Witness the steamships as early as page 7 of *Clockwork Angel*. Witness the carriage, the sound of horses' hooves and the "man reading the newspaper under a gas lamp" on page 29. Indeed, the opening scene of *Clockwork Angel* takes place on squalid streets in "cramped slums." The smells are Industrial Revolution: "smoke and rope and tar," and the streets are filled with "gambling hells, opium dens, and brothels" (*Clockwork Angel,* page 2). We're clearly in the steampunk subgenre, but we're also in a fantasy world where Shadowhunters, steles, iratzes, and demons exist.

Steampunk, like fantasy, lets readers dream about escaping into another time and place, in this case, a simpler time when technology was far more basic and innocent. Of course, in The Infernal Devices, the fantasy is charged with evil technology in the form of automata formed from copper, brass, and human parts, but the battle is age-old, that between good and evil rather than the rise of technologies we no longer understand or can hope to escape. Today, we have Big Brother; no Internet privacy; government monitoring of our whereabouts (video cameras are on street corners, in stores, and where we work), our activities (what we buy on the Internet is closely monitored), our health (medical records are routinely computerized and everyone from your dental hygienist to a random new doctor can view your life history), and our very lives (marriages, divorces, births of children, work histories, school records, home purchases). Back in simpler times, at least in epic fantasies, we battle satanic demons, pure evil, and the threat is age-old and simple compared to what we face today. If our heroes and heroines successfully destroy the demons and the Mortmain/de Quincey clockwork armies, then there's hope for living happily ever after. The battle lines are clearly drawn. Today, can you even define the enemy that represents evil? Is it your own government? Is it a mix of foreign governments? Is it even government at all, or rather, is it some type of global terrorism? Is it technology itself? Does anyone know anymore?

In the steampunk time of The Infernal Devices, there is no knowledge, much less threat, of nuclear warfare and chemical-biological weapons, minute entities that creep into our bodies, take over, and kill slowly, entities such as man-made viruses and other contagions. In Victorian times, people didn't worry that daily life would change dramatically overnight as ice caps melted and apocalypse hit us all. The Victorian era of The Infernal Devices was long before the mechanized and world-wide holocausts of future wars. It came before the two world wars, before Stalin's slaughters, before Chairman Mao, and before Vietnam. Of course, The Infernal Devices is *in* the time of Chairman Meow, but that's another story entirely!

Along with steam power, a mainstay of the steampunk movement is clockwork devices. No electronics, no computer chips, no integrated circuits, no Internet, no cable, no television, but plenty of intricate clockwork devices. Instead of today's little gray boxes and handheld cell phones, the steampunk era has huge steam-powered ships and engines, gleaming brass and copper, and polished mahogany. The allure is in the beauty and magnificence, the simplicity, all set in shadows. This is steampunk. This is fantasy. And this is *Clockwork Angel* and *Clockwork Prince*.

Another appeal of steampunk is its rejection of modern consumerism. The allure of glamour inherent in Victorian England, when the British Empire employed Shadowhunters to defend it from demons, is still evident in today's real world, where people worldwide remain fascinated by the British royals. People are sick of advertisements and the bombardment of commercials. People are weary of greedy modern corporations that always find new ways to suck our hard-earned wages from us. People feel suffocated by the many hundreds of regulations, tiny rules, and silly laws that make no sense to us. Seriously, who does *not* know that modern television commercials about cigarette companies doing good in the world are idiotic methods of making people think these companies are operating in our best interests rather than trying to sell tobacco products to teenagers? Steampunk allows us to escape from all this nonsense. Its time period is much more elegant and simple. Clary and Tessa aren't bombarded with and don't have to deal with all the nonsense that today's teenage girls experience every day. They don't have to eat diet yogurts and suck down diet drinks. They don't have to wear all the latest fashions just to be accepted by their friends. They don't have to listen to a million rules set down by adults. They aren't under the thumbs of an adult society, not really. They operate independently, together, to save society for both adults and children. They are at the forefront of decision making and battling evil. Try telling Will what to do, and good luck with that!

The period of The Infernal Devices comes on the heels of

literary greats such as Mary Shelley and Bram Stoker, books in which Gothic horrors such as the Frankenstein monster and Dracula sprang to life. In Mary Shelley's 1818 book, a scientist plays God and tries to reanimate bits and pieces of human life rolled into one cobbled creature, the Frankenstein monster. In The Infernal Devices, Mortmain and de Quincey cobble together bits and pieces of human life, as harvested by the Dark Sisters, into reanimated creatures called the clockwork armies or the automata. These bits and pieces are bound by copper wires and all sorts of mechanical devices. They're like a steampunk Terminator-Frankenstein set in Victorian England. Although I explore the automata in detail in an earlier chapter, it's worth noting here that in 1868, Edward S. Ellis published a novel called *The Steam Man of the Prairies,* in which the Steam Man is a steam-powered robot. The hero of the story, a teenager, used his Steam Man to go on adventures in the Wild West. Like Frankenstein's monster, Ellis's Steam Man was a precursor to the automata in The Infernal Devices.

As for fandom, it's huge and growing. In March 2013, Tucson, Arizona, hosted the Wild Wild West SteamPunk Convention and Gettysburg, Pennsylvania, hosted Steampunk at Gettysburg: Rewind Time. In April, there was the Steampunk Empire Symposium in Cincinnati, Ohio. In May, the Southern California Steampunk & Victoriana Convention Gaslight Gathering III: The Seven Seas took place in San Diego. Then there's ClockWork Alchemy in San Jose, California, the Steampunk World's Fair in Piscataway, New Jersey, and of course, Steamcon in Bellevue, Washington. And the list goes on . . . If you're interested in attending a steampunk gathering, go to steampunkis.org/forum/index.php?topic=224.0 for an extensive list.

A sub-subgenre of science fiction and fantasy, clockpunk is under the umbrella of steampunk. In clockpunk, intricate clockwork devices are the most prominent technology—instead of, say, steam-powered trains and airships. Quite often, the devices do amazing things that would be impossible scientifically because winding up a device wouldn't supply sufficient power. And clockpunk frequently features clockwork creatures, as do The Infernal Devices. Other examples in literature include:

- *Pasquale's Angel* by Paul J. McAuley, in which Leonardo da Vinci is an engineer rather than an artist in clockpunk Florence
- Clockwork Earth series by Jay Lake, mostly steampunk but includes the radical idea that the solar system is a huge clockwork device
- *Deathscent* by Robin Jarvis, in which Elizabethan robots are powered by clockwork and liquid technologies

Oddly enough, K. W. Jeter wrote a clockpunk novel in 1987 called *Infernal Devices.* The story takes place in London and involves human-fish hybrids and a brilliant clockwork maker whose father had been experimenting with building automata, clockwork humans. There are huge differences, of course, between the *Infernal Devices* book and The Infernal Devices series. For example, Jeter's hero winds up with an automaton twin of himself with amazing musical and sexual talents. No angels, no demons, no Shadowhunters.

I tend to write and read stories that interest me, just as you do. And I don't care which "punk" it's in, I only care if the story's good. Writers want to produce stories that are interesting and fun to read. Every reader wants to find good stories that grip us. So while The Infernal Devices by Cassandra Clare falls loosely into steampunk and clockpunk, what I really care about is that it's an epic read.

RESURRECTING THE DEAD AND LIVING FOREVER

The idea of resurrection is key to The Mortal Instruments series. When Jace dies and then is raised—resurrected—he's born a second time, with all of his protections stripped away and leaving him open to demonic attack. At the end of *City of Lost Souls,* the fifth book, he is "born again" as an angelic entity, something far more beautiful and powerful than a Shadowhunter. So not only does he rise from death, he later is reborn as what the reader perceives to be a savior. The idea of resurrection in Jace's case is very similar to resurrection in Christian theology. If you can resurrect the dead, doesn't it mean that everyone has the potential to be immortal?

I'm in the camp that believes in the simple process of birth, life, and death. No afterlife, not even the survival of the soul for eternity. We all die. It's inevitable.

However, people in all cultures throughout time, regardless of religion and ethnicity, have believed in life after death. For many, it's hard to imagine the cold, hard door of death leading to flat-out nothingness. They hope and believe that their souls, some essential spirit inside of them, will exist beyond the grave. It's how this happens, and whether we're resurrected in soul and/or body, that differs from culture to culture. It's a source of confusion for most of us.

Like many of us, Jem believes some of the myths about the afterlife but doesn't believe in others: "I believe the soul is eternal. But I don't believe in the fiery pit, the pitchforks, or endless torment. I don't believe you can threaten people into goodness" (*Clockwork Angel,* page 175). Will has different beliefs, just as people in the real world disagree about what happens when we die. He seems to be in the camp that believes in dust to dust: "I believe we are dust and shadows. What else is there?" (*Clockwork Angel,* page 175).

In some cultures, people worship the dead and request their help. Ghosts can appear and either help us or hurt us. In this way of thinking, if we pray to the dead, maybe we'll keep them happy with us and avoid harm. In The Mortal Instruments, Isabelle actually dates a ghost. In The Infernal Devices, Will is one of the Shadowhunters with the ability to hear ghosts talk, plead, weep, and wail. As *Clockwork Prince* opens, he encounters Old Molly, who seeks a piece of her past so she can finally die. We assume that Old Molly and these other ghosts are in a state of purgatory of some kind because they're all miserable, seeking talismans that will finally release them from ghost to death. In this case, we assume that the ghosts aren't quite dead yet.

Traditionally, in our culture, we think of a ghost as the spirit

of a dead person, but the ancients viewed a ghost as a disem-
bodied soul. The ancients thought that when people died, their
souls went to an underworld. Views about souls in the underworld differ quite a bit across cultures. For example, the Mela-
nesians believed that the soul divided into the aunga, the good
part, and the adaro, the ghostly bad part. The adaro returned to
the live body's home on a ship of the dead, or sometimes the
adaro simply scooted across the ground until reaching its destination. In The Mortal Instruments, with the Mark of Death on
him, Jace passes "beyond the Portal into the shadow realms,"
where his soul is "untethered" from his body (*City of Fallen
Angels,* pages 268–269). Here, in the underworld or shadow
realms, Jace's soul can return to his body only through necromancy, black magic, or the divine grace of an angel of God,
who uses its right hand to put the soul back.

I'm not sure why Jace doesn't return for a while as a ghost,
given that the ghostly domain serves as a sort of purgatory for
the dead en route to final death. Could it be that Jace goes directly to final death without a stop in purgatory ghostland?

In many cultures, ghosts appear in order to give living
people critical information. Old Molly does this for Will in the
Infernal Instruments. In real-world mythology, other ghosts
return to reenact their deaths. Does this happen in The Infernal Devices? Well, think about Tessa, who can change into
the dead and reenact their deaths. This seems very similar,
doesn't it?

The idea in The Infernal Devices of a purgatory or prison-
like place—where ghosts dwell—along the way from death to
final death is very common throughout world cultures. Typically, these way stations are gloomy and bleak, just as they
seem to be for the ghosts in The Infernal Devices. Examples are
Ananka and Sheol, which I'll describe momentarily.

But not all way stations and worlds of the dead are places of misery and suffering. Many cultures think the dead get lucky and survive eternally in happy, sunny locations forever. Examples are Valhalla and Tir na nÓg.

For the most part, cultures that believe in the afterlife also believe in the notion of purgatory, a horrible nowhere nothing state where we remain after death before going to a heavenly place or a terrible hell, a place where judges will determine our eternal "resting place."

In what is now Iraq near the Persian Gulf, the ancient Sumerians wrote on clay tablets about the afterlife and the world of the dead some four thousand years ago. Loosely known as the Mesopotamians, a wide swath of cultures in the Middle East believed the Sumerian ideas about the afterlife. These people included the Akkadians, who conquered the Sumerians, the Babylonians, and the Assyrians, and their ideas included common motifs in stories about purgatory and the afterlife: rivers, boatmen, gates with guardians. The story of Gilgamesh is one of the most famous of the Mesopotamian beliefs about purgatory and the afterlife.

In short, the Mesopotamian gods are thought to live in a place called the Great Above, and the Sumerians called the Queen of Heaven and Earth Inanna, while the Akkadians called her Isthar, the Assyrians called her Astarte, and the Phoenicians called her Ashtoreth. The dead remain forever in the Great Below in the Land of No Return, which is ruled by the goddess Ereshkigal. Finally, the source of humanity, one human male and one human female, is in an Eden called the Isle of the Blest beyond the Mountains of Mashu.

The Infernal Devices mentions heaven and hell, though the characters don't travel there, nor do ghosts speak of these places. When, in The Mortal Instruments, Jace dies and then returns, he doesn't remember a place of purgatory, much less learning or hearing anything about heaven or hell. We see only slight references, such as the "clockwork army, born of neither Heaven nor Hell" on page 240 of *Clockwork Angel*. Clary reminds Jace that love is "stronger than Heaven or Hell" on page 362 of *City of Fallen Angels*. The Angel Raziel tells Simon about Archangel Michael, commander of heaven's armies on page 428 of *City of Lost Souls*. And apparently, Michael's sword will strike down someone with more of hell in him than heaven. Repeatedly, we're told that blades forged in heaven or hell can fight pure evil. Further, there's a slight reference about blades that are "forged in the blackness of the Pit," which is a distinct reference to hell (*City of Lost Souls*, pages 192–193). Other clues about heaven are distinct references to the "palaces of Heaven" built from adamas (*City of Lost Souls*, page 368). And of course, there are a few mentions of the Prince of Hell, Lucifer, and his second in command, the Greater Demon Azazel. So while we don't know what heaven and hell are actually like in these books, we know that they exist in their traditional forms. Heaven is a divine, pure, and beautiful place. Hell is a terrible pit of sin and horror.

These ideas about heaven and hell are prevalent in cultures everywhere in our real world. Typically, a hero or heroine travels into the world of the dead to save somebody and/or fulfill a quest.

The Mesopotamians believed that after death, all people traveled to the underworld, where they dwelled eternally as shadowy remnants of their human selves. Everyone ended up in Arulla, the underworld, as shadows or ghosts. Only the gods were truly immortal; everyone else became immortal merely as ghosts.

In the ancient Sumerian version of the quest to save someone from the world of the dead, the Queen of Heaven and Earth, Inanna, wants to travel to the Land of No Return to visit her sister, the Queen of the Great Below, Ereshkigal. Wearing jewels and exquisite clothing, she makes her way from one gate to the next to the next leading to the world of the dead. At each gate, a guardian removes her jewels and clothing, and by the time she's at the final gate—the seventh—she's naked.

But remember, Ereshkigal is the Queen of the Great Below, probably not an incredibly happy place. Not only does she force her sister to strip and give away all of her jewels and clothes, when Inanna finally shows up for her visit, Ereshkigal inflicts sixty miseries upon her sister, and indeed, other versions of the story have Ereshkigal hanging her sister on a stake.

Luckily, showing that it's always a good thing to have friends, Inanna's alive friends on Earth beseech the gods to release her from Ereshkigal's domain. With the condition that Inanna supply another person to dwell in Ereshkigal's world of the dead, Ereshkigal finally lets Inanna return to the world of the living.

And what forces Inanna to actually send a replacement human to this horrible place of the dead? Goblins. Bad goblins. Ereshkigal sends them to the world of the living, and they make Inanna do their bidding. Showing that it's always wise not to cheat on your lover, Inanna sends her cheating husband, Dumuzi, to Ereshkigal.

Inanna's actually a nice person, and she works out a sort of world-of-the-dead custody arrangement with Dumuzi. He's with Ereshkigal in the world of the dead for half the year, she's there for the second half of the year.

As for Gilgamesh, king of Uruk, he isn't content with a ghostly death. He wants to be truly immortal, and his quest is to find the secret of eternal life as possessed by the gods.

Like most epic heroes, including Jace, Gilgamesh is strong, brave, and arrogant. The gods create a friend for him known as Enkidu, a wild man living in the forest with the beasts. Gilgamesh, you see, represents human society, while Enkidu represents the natural world. To make a long story shorter, when the wild animals reject Enkidu, he goes to Uruk and fights Gilgamesh, but he finally surrenders and proclaims Gilgamesh as his king. Eventually, the two men become extremely close friends.

After fighting a forest monster, the gods inflict Enkidu with a fatal illness, and he has a nightmare about Arulla, which is all *shadows and dust*. Gilgamesh is horrified and doesn't want to end up in Arulla, place of eternal misery. Gilgamesh seeks an immortal human about whom he's heard stories, and he travels to the world of the dead, where the immortal first warns him but then tells him that he must find a secret plant of immortality that grows at the bottom of the sea. After traveling through the Mountains of Mashu in bleak darkness, Gilgamesh encounters a boatman and the sea, and the boatman tells him that the rest of the journey will be hopeless. And it is hopeless, for while Gilgamesh does indeed find the plant of immortality and does indeed snatch it off the ocean floor, a snake grabs it from his hands and swims away. Gilgamesh's quest for immortality fails.

In the end, in the tale of Gilgamesh as well as in tales from ancient societies all over the world, we learn that for humans, death is inevitable. There is no immortality for us. We will die, and we will be nothing more than *shadows and dust*.

In The Infernal Devices, we have the Book of the White, which provides the magic required to bind or even unbind the soul from the body. This Book of the White might serve in many ways as the Book of the Dead in real cultures in ancient times. For example, the Sumerians had their clay tablets of the dead, and the Egyptians wrote their Book of the Dead on papyrus thirty-five hundred years ago. In this second case, the book included magic spells related to the dead in the underworld.

In the beginning, the Egyptians believed that only their nobility survived death. Later, in approximately 1570, the Egyptians wrote about their god of the dead, Osiris, who also judged anyone entering the world of the dead. Horus, who was Osiris's son, was god of all the living. Osiris himself was a sacrificed and resurrected god, similar to the idea of the Christian Jesus, who was sacrificed and resurrected.

In ancient Egypt, death rituals focused on preserving, dying, and wrapping the corpse and transforming it into a permanent mummy. These rituals were time-consuming, often requiring as much as seventy days for a skilled person to complete. The mummified corpse was the eternal home of the deceased person's soul, and the priests opened the mummy's mouth so the soul could "breathe" in and out forever.

But the Egyptians' idea of soul wasn't quite the same as that of other cultures. They separated the ka, the life force, from the ba, the soul. The ka, as an extended part of what the Egyptians considered divine energy, was connected to the animation, the life force, of the gods. Symbolizing the vital essence of the person, the ka was portrayed as two arms, and because it remain connected to the gods, after a person died, the ka lived on.

As for the ba, this was an individual soul that supplied the person with his own consciousness. The soul in The Mortal Instruments is critical to a person's life force because, like the ba, it is the source of free will. Remember, in *City of Lost Souls,* we learn that the parabatai binds the souls of two people but leaves their free will intact, but Lilith's twinning ritual is demonic because it "removes the free will of the secondary partner in the spell" (*City of Lost Souls,* page 192). The free will is critical, we're told, because it is "what makes us Heaven's creatures" (ibid.).

The Egyptian ba, symbolized as a bird with a human head, could fly to and from the dead body, and if glorified in death as an akh, or transfigured spirit, it could even fly between the world of the dead and the human world of the living. This

STRONG ABS ARE ALWAYS A GOOD THING

Closely associated with the ka, the ba, and the akh was the Egyptian ab, or moral conscience. Symbolized by the human heart, the ab was required for the afterlife judgment of the deceased person.

Although the divine pharaohs were mummified during the Old Kingdom, later on, rich Egyptians who could afford mummification also went through the process upon death. The pharaohs ascended to Re, the sun god in the sky, but the others had to be judged after death before shuttling to their eternal rest homes, so to speak.

In a Hall of Justice in the house of Osiris, the Lord of the Dead, the ka and ba both received white garments and sandals to wear. A former king of Egypt, Osiris was descended from the gods, but during his reign, his evil brother Seth cut Osiris into fourteen pieces, which he then scattered throughout the land of Egypt. Osiris's wife and sister, Isis, was heartbroken and hunted for all of the amputated body parts, and then like a child trying to put Humpty Dumpty back together again, she put her dead husband back together.

And now for the really interesting part. It worked. By putting the dismembered body parts back together, Isis was able to re-create Osiris sufficiently to conceive and then give birth to his son, Horus. And then in true epic form, Horus went out and killed Seth to avenge the death of his father. And off went Osiris to rule the world of the dead as its king and god.

This may be why the Egyptians began mummifying their pharaohs. Remember, Isis preserved Osiris's body, and mummification preserved the bodies of subsequent pharaohs from decomposition. In fact, the priestly rituals during the mummification funerals included the reenacting of the preservation and restoration of Osiris's body parts into one whole body. Before others could enter Osiris's kingdom of the dead, Osiris had to judge the person's life and rule on the fate of his eternal soul.

(continued)

First, the god of wisdom, Thoth, attempted to prosecute the dead person for crimes committed during life. If the soul passed Thoth's scrutiny, it went to Osiris, who put the dead person's heart on a scale of justice. This heart probably symbolized the ab. Osiris weighed the heart against a feather given to him by Ma'at, the goddess of truth, who represented justice and righteousness, the ultimate order of the cosmos. All around the scales of justice sat the gods of the dead. Anubis with his jackal head adjusted the scales, and Thoth with his ibis head was the one who would inscribe the soul's judgment. Am-mut, sometimes written as Ammit, lurked to the side, ready to consume the heart. Am-mut, eater of the dead, had a lion's body, a crocodile's jaws, and a hippopotamus's rear end. If the heart, representing the dead person's moral conscience, sank lower than Ma'at's feather, then Am-mut leapt forward and ate the corpse's heart, and the dead person wasn't allowed to go the lovely world of the dead where Osiris ruled.

If the heart weighed the same as or less than the feather, meaning that the dead person led a moral and decent life, then Osiris allowed the dead person's life force and soul into the world of the dead.

Upon entry into Osiris's realm, the dead person was somewhat resurrected in a new body clad in white clothing and sandals. Using the Egyptian Book of the Dead, which contained spells to protect him from monsters, from suffocation, and even from dying again, the dead person attempted to transform into a new earthly form, such as a bird, a snake, or a flower.

With strong abs, the dead could be resurrected. This is much like in The Mortal Instruments, where, barring the use of forbidden and evil necromancy, the only way to be resurrected after death and get your human soul back is by "an Angel of God's own right hand" (*City of Fallen Angels,* page 269). An angel of God isn't going to breathe your soul back into your dead body if you're evil. He's going to do this for you only if you've led a morally decent life.

means it was able to enter and leave what The Mortal Instruments series loosely terms the shadow realms. In The Mortal Instruments, upon death, Jace's soul leaves his body and he goes into the shadow realms.

The Sumerians and Egyptians weren't the only ancient cultures believing in the afterlife and the land of the dead. Also in the Middle East, the prophet Zoroaster brought a religion that became known as Zoroastrianism, which spread to India, Russia, and the eastern Balkans. This religion, which scholars think began between 1400 and 1200 BC, remained very popular until the seventh century AD.

The sacred book of Zoroastrianism, called Avesta, teaches that two gods exist, the good one known as Ahura Mazda, and the evil one known as Angra Mainyu. Ahura Mazda lives in the heavens with seven angels, while Angra Mainyu lives in an underworld with his demons in dark hell. The two gods, good versus evil, battle forever for human souls.

According to Zoroastrianism, after death, the human soul remains near the body for three days while the god Mithra, along with Rashnu, the angel of justice, judges the soul. They determine the eternal fate of the person's soul by a bridge that leads to the world of the dead. The morally good person gets lucky and goes with the beautiful Daena across the bridge into a house of song. The morally bad person immediately goes to hell. Mithra and Rashnu weighed all the good acts of a person's entire lifetime against all the bad acts. It took only a surplus balance of three bad acts against good ones to cast a person's soul into hell forever. If the person's good deeds exactly equaled his bad deeds, then the soul entered purgatory forever. There was no release from Zoroastrian purgatory. No house of song in the future. Just nothing.

Possibly the most famous shadow realm is the kingdom of Hades, which was ruled by the Greek god of the underworld, conveniently called Hades. With his brothers, Zeus and Poseidon, Hades defeated his father, Cronus, in a battle, and then divided the world into three parts. Zeus ruled the earth, Poseidon ruled the seas, and Hades ruled the land of the dead. Hades then divided his kingdom into many regions, including Tartarus, where the evil dead go to be tortured for eternity. Probably due to the evil nature of Tartarus, Hades is often a synonym for hell. Every soul not in eternal hell exists forever as a ghostly shadow. You have to wonder about the god Hades, who could have taken the earth or the seas instead of hell. He must have been a sadistic fellow to want hell as his kingdom.

In Hades, the ghostly souls are called shades and represent shadows of their former living selves. Like all shadow realms, Hades is dark, murky, and bleak.

In later years, the Greeks believed that Hades included an earthly paradise called Elysium, and a hell called Dis, which contained levels of hell with Tartarus being the worst.

So we can see some parallels between ancient religious beliefs of the afterlife and resurrection with those of The Mortal Instruments and The Infernal Devices. But the Shadowhunter stories play strongly off Western religious ideas, which themselves grew from the earlier traditions.

Long ago, the Israelites lived between the Jordan River and the Mediterranean, and they were under constant threat of extinction unless they converted to other religions. Between the ninth century BC and the second century AD, the Israelites developed the Five Books of Moses, the Torah, otherwise known as the Old Testament or Hebrew Bible. In the second century, the Romans massacred the Jewish culture, and many of these ancient Jews assimilated ideas about the afterlife into their religion for centuries.

Some ancient Jews thought the world had an earthly component as well as a heaven and a netherworld. The living could talk to the dead in the netherworld, which also happened to house demons, and request help. They could also ask for help from the sky gods in heaven. These ideas withered away in Judaism for fairly obvious reasons. For one thing, the basic tenet of the Jewish faith is the belief in One God and Only One God. Simon Lewis could tell you that the Shema prayer plastered all over his mother's door is the most basic Jewish prayer, "Hear, O Israel, the Lord is our God, the Lord is One." Following the Shema comes another key sentence, "Blessed be the Name of His Glorious Kingdom forever and ever."

Most Jews in the ancient world—as well as today—believed that we don't communicate with the dead. We don't seek help from the dead, we don't worship the dead. We respect the dead and honor our ancestors, but even Moses isn't viewed as a saint or a god. He was a great man, a prophet, someone God trusted with the Ten Commandments, but he wasn't a godhead. Jews worshipped only the one God, who demanded total obedience at all times. This is the more traditional concept of Judaism.

Another belief of the ancient Jews was that dead souls would be granted immortality, that all the people who suffer terribly in life will finally find happiness after death. This ancient Jewish belief led to the more traditional Christian view of the afterlife.

By the eighteenth century, scholars began referring to the ancient Assyrians, Babylonians, Canaanites, Phoenicians, and early Hebrews as Semites. Other cultures, such as the Sumerians, Egyptians, Hittites, and Persians, had different views from the Semites. Although the Hebrews later rejected the earlier Semitic beliefs about the afterlife, these ideas provided a foundation for Christianity's approach to what happens after we die.

The Semitic netherworld, called Sheol, was a pit beneath the ground, where dead people were ghostly images of their former living selves. It was a place from which there was no escape. For example, Job describes what will happen to him when he dies and descends into Sheol: "Before I go to the place of no return, to the land of gloom and deep shadow; a land of darkness, as darkness itself; and of the shadow of the death, without any order, and where the light is as darkness" (Job 10:21–22).

Ancient Semites buried the dead in dirt or placed the corpses in underground vaults. They wanted the dead to be in the closest contact with Sheol, believing that as the body decomposed, the shadowy ghost soul of the dead person left the body and traveled down to the netherworld.

The dead whose lives had been righteous and morally good survived eternally in the upper level of Sheol, where the living could more easily communicate with them. The dead whose lives had been morally deficient dwelled forever in the lowest realms of Sheol, where it was much more difficult, if not impossible, to help their descendants.

Early biblical references to resurrection include:

"Many of those who sleep in the dust of the Earth will awake, some to everlasting life, others to shame and everlasting contempt" (Daniel 12:2). The Book of Daniel predicted a terrible time, when resurrection would occur, including judgment of the dead, probably based on a Book of Life.

"Thus says the Lord God, Behold, I will open your graves and raise you from them . . . I will put my Spirit in you and you will live" (Ezekiel 37:12, 14). It's possible that this passage refers to restoring the Israelite nation as a unified people rather than resurrecting the individual dead. However, the passage could be taken literally.

"But your dead will live, their bodies will rise. You who dwell in the dust, wake up and shout for joy. The Earth will give birth to the dead" (Isaiah 26:19).

"O Lord, You brought me up from the grave. You spared me from going down into the pit" (Psalms 30:3).

From earliest times, the Christian religion looked to the death and resurrection of Jesus, their savior. In the New Testament, we learn of Jesus's trial, of his torture and his death, his ascent to a heavenly throne, and also of his return to life. As Jace dies and then is born again as what the reader hopes will be the savior of the Shadowhunters and the Downworlders, so Jesus was seen as the divine agent, the son of God, who would provide human salvation. In Mark 1:15, Jesus talks about the arrival of the kingdom of God, and in the first century, the early Christians viewed Jesus as the Lord of this kingdom. Saul of Tarsus converted to become the Christian missionary Paul, and he taught that those who worshipped Jesus as the key to their divine salvation would go to heaven, and indeed, at the time of the Second Coming of Christ, these people would be resurrected. In the New Testament, Paul says that those who will not get into the kingdom of God include unrepentant idolaters, adulterers, thieves, sorcerers, swindlers, and fornicators, as well as those who are indecent, who quarrel with others, and who are greedy. He also adds that homosexuals won't be allowed into the kingdom of God, either. In The Mortal Instruments, should Jace evolve into a savior of sorts in future books, probably he will include homosexuals in whatever new "kingdom" exists. The series has a lot of good homosexual characters, including Magnus Bane and Alec. While some parents in these books fear homosexuality—or at least their gay children think their parents disapprove—the Shadowhunters don't seem to care at all one way or the other.

Not only did the early Christians believe that Jesus would be resurrected from the dead, but they also looked to him as the judge of those who are in the world of the dead. In the Book of Revelation, Jesus is the divine judge of who will be saved and who will go to hell forever.

John writes about the battle between good and evil, between God and Satan. In John's time, the Roman Empire was considered a satanic evil. John focuses on a vision of heaven and earth coinciding, and he's more interested in the beauty and splendors in heaven than in hell and damnation. John says that he visited heaven thanks to an angel, and there he saw God in human form on a divine throne more awe inspiring, gorgeous, and dazzling than all the jewels in the world. While spirits guarded God's throne, angels were everywhere, singing, "Holy, holy, holy is the Lord God Almighty; he was, he is, and he is to come." According to John, twenty-four elders were in heaven with God, correlating to the twenty-four families of Jewish priests in those days. As John watched, more angels flocked to God and His throne, and then Jesus Christ appeared. As he continued to watch, transfixed, John saw 144,000 people representing every tribe of Israel, and he also saw an almost infinite number of people representing all religions, tribes, races, and nations on Earth. John writes that a heavenly elder tells him that all of these people he sees are martyrs who died for the sake of Christianity.

John's apocalyptic vision began with the unlocking of a scroll, or book, that had been secured with seven seals. The first four seals showed visions of four horses in battle, with Death riding the fourth horse. The fifth seal showed the vision of all the Christian martyrs who, according to John, wanted their killers to be judged as sinners. The sixth seal showed the end of time, in which the moon became blood, the sun went black, and earthquakes split across the entire world. And finally, the seventh seal was a vision of total silence. This apocalyptic vision involving the seven seals would avenge the death of the Christian martyrs via resurrection and judgment of all the dead. The entire world would change as a result, and the weak would inherit the earth.

How does The Mortal Instruments use Revelation and this entire apocalyptic vision? For one thing, during a discussion of Lot's wife and two guys turning into pillars of salt, we are told that "whosoever slayeth Cain, vengeance shall be taken on him sevenfold" (*City of Fallen Angels,* page 123). Later, when Simon is fighting Lilith, she whispers "sevenfold" and then turns into salt that disappears (*City of Fallen Angels,* page 388). John's Apocalypse includes seven trumpets and seven vials of wrath dumped upon the world to cause complete destruction, after which all the kings will gather at Armageddon. The sevenfold vengeance mentioned in *City of Fallen Angels* may relate to the seven vials of wrath, the seven trumpets, and the seven seals.

And much later in the series, Sebastian tells Clary about the Seventh Sacred Site, which she later tells Simon that she thinks is a Portal-like tomb through which demons emerge into the world. Again, something essential is *sevenfold.* The reader wonders if the Seventh Sacred Site is related to John's apocalyptic vision, to Armageddon. This isn't explained in the first seven books of The Mortal Instruments and The Infernal Devices, and perhaps we'll discover what Cassandra Clare has up her sleeve in a later installment of the story. But for now, we know from Magnus Bane that there are Seven Sacred Sites, and at each location, ley lines meet, making magic much more powerful. He also says that the Seventh Sacred Site mentioned by Sebastian and then Clary is indeed a tomb that's in Ireland.

John also describes how the Archangel Michael and his angels fight Satan and all the demons. After the forces of light defeat the forces of darkness, says John, God will establish an eternal kingdom in which all souls will live forever in peace. As John writes, "I saw the souls of them that were beheaded for the witness of Jesus, and for the word of God, and which had not worshipped the beast, neither his image, neither had received his mark upon their foreheads, or in their hands; and they lived and reigned with Christ a thousand years" (Revelation 20:4). After this thousand years, and at long last, Satan, his demons, and all evil would be completely destroyed. Then Christ would perform a second resurrection of all the dead, and Christ would judge them.

Of course, in The Mortal Instruments series, as forces of light, the Shadowhunters need the Archangel Michael's sword to battle the forces of darkness. Along with epic romance, these books are about the battle between good and evil, light and darkness.

As mentioned earlier, other than the intervention of a powerful angel, the only way for a soul to return to its human body in The Mortal Instruments and The Infernal Devices is through necromancy, a very dark magic. But necromancy also includes wiring biological organs and flesh with clockwork mechanisms and then trying to infuse the resulting creatures with demonic energies. This is what the Dark Sisters have been trying to do, as evidenced by what Will and Jem encounter when seeking Mrs. Dark. They find dark magic remnants, including a pentagram, bloody knives, animal parts, and pools of blood. According to Mortmain, Mrs. Dark brings Mrs. Black back to life using a necromantic charm.

But necromancy also includes communicating with the dead. As I noted before, isn't this what Tessa Gray does when she Changes into dead people and their voices are in her mind?

King Saul in the Old Testament asks a necromancer, a wizard who specializes in communicating with the dead, to tell him the outcome of a battle that hasn't happened yet. The necromancer joins the world of the living with Sheol by digging a hole in the ground. The shadow ghost of the prophet Samuel emerges from the hole and tells the necromancer that King Saul will die in battle the following day. According to Samuel, the dead are already waiting for the arrival of King Saul's shadow in Sheol. King Saul dies just as predicted by the dead Samuel through the necromancer. In later times, biblical scholars denounced necromancy as pagan rituals.

13

ALCHEMY AND OUROBOROS

Alchemy plays a big role in The Infernal Devices. On the surface, it may not seem as if this is the case, but if you think about it for a while, you'll see that what Mortmain, de Quincey, and the Dark Sisters are trying to do is transmute matter from one nature to another. The classic idea is that alchemy turns base metals such as tin and lead into gold and silver. But alchemy is much more than a method of getting rich via magical pseudochemistry. It also is a magical way of bestowing an elixir of youth and even immortality, as evidenced by Mortmain who, according to Charlotte, probably used "black magic to prolong [his life]" (*Clockwork Prince*, page 149). This is why a mundane, Mortmain—who isn't even a paranormal creature with magical powers—appears to be forty years old although he is actually seventy-five.

Alchemy also involves thinking of all of nature as one unified "thing" that alchemical wizards can shuffle and interchange. A main goal of alchemy is to unify, to understand and bring together all the mysteries of creation, life, and death. This notion, of course, is central to The Infernal Devices, in which Mortmain wants to alter the nature of life itself. Transforming lead into gold is just an offshoot of the real objectives of alchemy.

The ouroboros, representing the eternal unity of everything and the cycle of birth-death-rebirth, is an ancient alchemical symbol of a snake eating its tail. The snake is in a circle so its head meets the end of the tail. Inside the circular snake is our world, and the rest of the universe and all other dimensions lie outside. Psychologist Carl Jung viewed the alchemical ouroboros as representing immortality as well as the idea of a human assimilating his own shadow self in a feedback process, birth to death to rebirth.

In The Infernal Devices, the Pyxis contains demonic energy (a form of demon pseudosoul) and is emblazoned with the symbol of the ouroboros, which also serves as the symbol of the Pandemonium Club. Sometimes, the ouroboros apparently comes in double form, at least in *Clockwork Angel,* where on page 5, Jem shows Will a misericord dagger with two snakes, which Jem says symbolizes both the end and then the beginning of the world. It's interesting to note that Jem first refers to the end of the world rather than the beginning, which leads me to think that the end of the world in this series might be like an apocalypse of sorts, the end of life as we know it, and then we'll have a new beginning as Jace rises in his new angelic form and defeats all evil.

Just as religious elements infuse The Mortal Instruments and The Infernal Devices, they also infuse real-world alchemical ideas. Think about the ouroboros itself. It's a serpent and one of the most common alchemical symbols. The ancient Egyptians used the ouroboros symbol some sixteen centuries before Christ to signify eternal regeneration of life-death-life, the unity of all things everywhere. Ecclesiastical buildings often included alchemical symbols and paintings, even the "existence, in 1652, of an alchemical painting upon the wall of Westminster Abbey and . . . an alchemical window, symbolising in colour the preparation of the [Philosopher's] Stone."[1] Experts further suggest that alchemical symbols represent the resurrection and judgment day, as well as the mystery of mankind's future (ibid.).

In approximately 350 BC, Aristotle taught that matter is continuous, and hence, he said, we can divide matter into infinite pieces. This idea didn't evolve for a long time beyond the notion of atomic matter differing in size, shape, and form. Scholars believe that alchemy, a magical precursor to chemistry, arose in Mesopotamia and then spread to Egypt and Greece, and from there, to China and India.

Right before the time of The Infernal Devices, the German chemist Justus von Liebig, who lived between 1803 and 1873, claimed that alchemy was a prechemistry from the Middle Ages. A common example is that, in medieval times, alchemists believed that joining impure sulfur and mercury under certain planetary influences would yield base metals such as tin and lead. Joining pure sulfur and mercury would yield gold. And even more, joining superpure sulfur and mercury would yield something called the philosopher's stone, which could then directly turn base metals into gold and silver. Some people thought the philosopher's stone could also bestow immortality and longevity of the kind enjoyed by Mortmain.

The earliest symbols of alchemy denoted the four elements and the seven known metals. Fire was represented by a triangle

KHEM AND AL-KHEMIA

In ancient Egypt, Khem was the god of fertility and reproduction who controlled the fertility of all nature, including the dark soil near the Nile River. The Egyptians believed in life after death, and so they developed mummification processes, which required basic knowledge of chemistry. Related to the idea of fertility is immortality through reproduction.

When Alexander the Great conquered Egypt, the Greeks started to explore the Egyptian ideas about Khem, immortality, and chemistry. The Greeks believed in four basic elements: fire, earth, air, and water, and they merged their beliefs with the divine scientific practices in Egypt. They referred to Egypt as Khemia.

The Arabs conquered Egypt in the seventh century, and they added the prefix *al-*, meaning "the" to *Khemia.* They referred to Egypt as al-Khemia, or the black land.

In the sixteenth century in Europe, alchemists were in two camps. One experimented with chemical compounds and reactions, eventually becoming what is now called chemistry. The other focused on the magical or more metaphysical aspects of alchemy, seeking an elixir of youth, immortality, and a way to turn lead into gold. In 1661, Robert Boyle published *The Sceptical Chymist,* which disproved the four-elements theory of alchemy.

By the time of The Infernal Devices, the science of chemistry was robust. In 1803, John Dalton published his atomic theory; in 1854, Heinrich Geissler invented the vacuum tube; in 1879, William Crookes discovered cathode rays; and in 1885, Eugene Goldstein discovered the proton.

pointing up, to suggest ascending particles of matter. Water was represented by a triangle pointing down, to suggest descending particles. Air, by an upward-pointing triangle with a horizontal line near the top, suggesting increased weight of ascending particles. Earth was represented by a downward-pointing triangle with a horizontal line near the base, suggesting increased weight of descending particles.

As for the seven classical metals of alchemy, they were all represented by planetary objects: gold by the sun, silver by the moon, copper by Venus, iron by Mars, tin by Jupiter, mercury by the planet Mercury, and lead by Saturn.

Alchemists ranged from complete quacks to philosophers, mystics, and visionaries. The quacks were charlatans and rogues who called themselves alchemists to sound more professional and respectable. Their objective, of course, was to cheat ordinary people out of their money by claiming, for example, that they could turn lead into gold. In fiction, it's this type of alchemist who appears most often—as a magician, a necromancer, or an astrologer. An example of a real-world alchemist quack was Simon Forman, who lived between 1552 and 1611. Forman indulged in necromancy and other forms of dark magic. Authorities imprisoned him repeatedly for defrauding the public, but despite this he eventually gained favor with London society ladies, who wanted his charms and love potions.

A step up from the charlatans, the puffers, also known as souffleurs, maintained a strong belief that elements could be transmuted, or changed, from one to another. They focused on finding new substances and discovering the basis of chemical phenomena.

In approximately 1520, Hans Weiditz, a famous artist of his time, produced a woodcutting that showed the medieval alchemist's laboratory. This image reminds me of the benches, tables, and tools in The Infernal Devices. If you have a local university library, ask if they have a copy of John Read's *Through Alchemy to Chemistry: A Procession of Ideas & Personalities*. Between pages 78 and 79 is a reproduction of Weiditz's woodcutting, and the author writes that "the equipment includes also an anvil, hammers, tongs, pincers, and other tools. Altogether the scene is reminiscent of an old-fashioned village smithy, rather than of a laboratory." He explains that this was the type of laboratory used by the quacks.

In the real world, by the time of The Infernal Devices, chemistry had basically replaced alchemy, although fringe elements of society still practiced the latter.

MEDIEVAL ALCHEMICAL "RULES"

Supposedly engraved on something called the Emerald Tablet in the tomb of Hermes Trismegistus were the rules of medieval alchemy. Some people believe Hermes was an Egyptian god who rules all the arts and sciences. The Emerald Tablet is well known among students of alchemy, and while it has never been found, people believe it defined the rules of nature, the creation of life, and the fundamental aspects of matter as unified across the span of the entire universe. Basically, the rules included ideas such as these:

- All that is below is like all that is above, one universal thing.
- One word of one Being created all things, and from the one universal thing came all else via adaptation.
- The sun is the universal thing's father, its mother is the moon, it lives in the wind, and the earth is its nurse.
- The universal thing is perfection.
- If you separate matter from matter, earth from fire, exercise great caution.

14

OF THEMES AND SCHEMES

Character, plot, and theme are all crucial to building novels that work. The next few chapters delve a little farther, hopefully in an entertaining way, into some basic literary analysis of The Mortal Instruments and The Infernal Devices. But don't worry, it won't be like reading a textbook!

For aspiring writers, this analytic approach to The Mortal Instruments and The Infernal Devices should get you thinking about how to write your own stories. Most important, for fans of The Mortal Instruments, this analysis should shed new light on how Cassandra Clare spins her magic tales.

The author includes many worldviews and lessons in her novels. What does her Mortal Instruments universe tell us about our real-world interactions? How do the plot and characters, as well as the tone of the novels, present and develop her themes? Are characters confronted with ethical decisions?

We all know from school that a theme is the worldview or main concern expressed in a novel or a series of novels. The three main components of good fiction are theme, character, and plot. Without all three, the story isn't particularly strong. Obviously, the story needs characters, but the strength of the overall work depends on how well the author draws the characters. The same is true for plot. I've read books in which characterization is shallow and the plot doesn't seem to exist. The character meanders through events, but the reader doesn't care much because she's not invested in the character as a human being, and he's not doing anything that she cares about. The final component, theme, ties into character motivations and the overall pull and tug of the plot.

Is it possible to write a novel without a theme?

Here's what I think. Every novel has a theme, even bad novels. The writer sits at the keyboard, creating her story, and as she works, she consciously decides to include or omit events, actions, descriptions, and dialogue. She's self-editing her work as she goes. She's also consciously thinking about events, actions, description, and dialogue to *add* to the story as she goes. The way she uses all of these tools reflects how she feels about the story, where it's heading, and what her characters are like. By using craft, or writing tools, the author expresses what is called the tone of the story, which may be dark, depressing, mellow, funny, sly, intellectual, intimate, condescending, serious, ironic, etc. This tone expresses the author's worldview. Hence, even a poorly written novel will have a theme of some kind. You may have to look for it, but it's in there.

I boiled down the main themes of The Mortal Instruments and The Infernal Devices into these groups:

- ▓ To thine own self be true
- ▓ Brute force hatred is not cool
- ▓ Good versus evil and light versus shadow
- ▓ Work together for the common good
- ▓ Love is a double-edged sword
- ▓ Women's lib

There are additional themes, but these are six major ones that I discovered in the text. All of these themes are dramatized. What I mean by that is: the author doesn't just write, "Oh, brute force hatred is not cool." She shows us the theme, that hatred isn't cool, by the actions and events in the novels.

TO THINE OWN SELF BE TRUE

Luke reveals this theme as early as page 23 of *City of Bones,* when he tells Clary, "There's nothing wrong with being different." Later, acting as a mentor and guide to Clary, he tells her on page 211 of *City of Ashes,* "What you're blaming yourself for is *being what you are.*" By going on to explain that she must be happy with who she is, that we all have the right to make our own choices, Luke underscores the theme that we must be true to ourselves.

This theme touches all of us because we all know what it's like to be tormented simply for being who we are. People might sneer and make fun of us, they might tell lies about us, but in the end, when you wake up in the morning and when you go to sleep at night, the only person who truly knows who you are and why you do what you do is, of course, *you.* You're the one who lives with your conscience. You can't please everyone, so why bother trying? There's always going to be somebody out there who gets joy out of putting you down. Ignore him or her. Be true to yourself.

It takes Alec a long time to figure this out. He tries very hard to hide the fact that he's gay, but everybody who's close to him already knows it anyway, and they accept him for who he is. They know he's okay, as is, before he knows it.

Clary notices how beautiful Isabelle is and thinks about it, makes comments about it, wishes that she, Clary, were more glamorous. Tessa feels all these things about Jessamine. Almost every teenage girl obsesses over what she looks like and what other girls look like, too. Almost every teenage girl wishes that she were more glamorous. But in the end, as for Clary and Tessa, being who you are is what truly matters, not what you look like. The surface veneer will loose its luster as you age, and it doesn't matter how gorgeous and slick you were in your youth, you're going to get old just like everybody else. The inside you is the *real* you.

Another morally decent character is Jem, but he too struggles with these issues, not quite comfortable in his own skin. As he explains on page 320 of *Clockwork Angel,* "When other Nephilim look at me, they see only a Shadowhunter. Not like mundanes, who look at me and see a boy who is not entirely foreign but not quite like them, either." Jem is telling us that it's easier to be accepted as a supernatural being than as an Asian person. Is our real world actually this bad?

Then there's poor Tessa, who doesn't even know *what* she is, *where* she came from, or *who* she is—talk about identity issues! It must be especially hard for Tessa to be true to herself given she knows so little about her background, but she does manage to remain morally decent and kind.

Charlotte and Sophie talk about this theme, that you have to be true to yourself, believe in who you are on the inside, hold your head high no matter what happens. Take a look at page 197 of *Clockwork Angel,* when Charlotte says to Tessa, "Sophie said to me once that she was glad she had been scarred. She said that whoever loved her now would love her true self, and not her pretty face." And Charlotte tells Tessa what I just told you, my readers, that "the power is who you are," that Tessa "must also love yourself." There is no clearer way to state this theme.

BRUTE FORCE HATRED IS NOT COOL

This is another big theme in The Mortal Instruments and The Infernal Devices series. We've all been hated by somebody at some point and probably for no reason that we know. But this particular theme is about what I think of as "brute force hatred," that is, the kind of illogical hatred of racists, Nazis, homophobes, and anyone else who hates other people because of race, religion, ethnicity, or sexual orientation. Of course, there are gray shades of everything. You can be uncomfortable about other people without being a racist, Nazi, or homophobe; but when the hatred is elevated to extremes—*to violent extremes*—it's incredibly bad. This is what Cassandra Clare is telling us, that the pure hatred of an entire class of people is wrong.

Valentine reminds me of a Nazi. He hates Downworlders simply because they *are* Downworlders. He doesn't view them as individual people. Talk about racism! He wants to build an army of super Shadowhunters who are on the side of evil. On page 79 of *City of Bones,* Hodge tells Clary that Valentine "despised Downworlders and felt that they should be slaughtered, wholesale, to keep this world pure for human beings." Doesn't this remind you of the Nazis?

As in our real world, the illogical hatred of one entire group of people stretches back seemingly forever. As Jace comments on page 196 of *City of Bones*, "A few hundred years of the Accords can't wipe out a thousand years of hostility." This reminds me of what goes on in the Middle East, where peace just never seems to happen.

Even among Downworlders themselves, there's illogical hatred between werewolves and vampires. Clary has to lecture Maia to get along with Simon—and all Downworlders— telling her that the two groups of Downworlders have to stop blaming each other. Think back, do you remember Maia's explanation of the strong ethnic hatred of werewolves for vampires, why Maia says werewolves and vampires can *never* be friends, no matter what? I'll give you a hint: what she says doesn't explain why, in our real world, ethnic groups blindly hate each other simply for existing.

And here's the answer. Remember that demons basically create both vampires and werewolves by infecting them with a demonic disease of some kind. So according to Maia, the demon group that created vampires was one species, while the demon group that created werewolves was another species. These demon species hate each other. Therefore, she explains that when it comes to vampires and werewolves, it's "in our blood to hate each other too. We can't help it" (*City of Ashes*, page 230).

Is it possible in real life for one ethnic population to hate another because it's "in the blood"? Not in real life, no. Nazis didn't have a set of genes that forced them to hate entire populations of other people and to think of them as subhuman. There is no such set of genes that causes any group of people to violently hate another group. Nor is there any infection or disease that causes such hatred. It's all in the head.

GOOD VERSUS EVIL AND LIGHT VERSUS SHADOW

This theme might be stated as good must prevail over evil. Every character struggles with his or her conscience and with difficult choices. This is true for all of us, as well, in the real world.

If you have a kind heart, how do you react when somebody accuses you of terrible things or acts in an unkind way to others? If you lash back, does that make you less good?

Suppose you think of yourself as a nice person who cares about others, someone who is good. Now suppose that you completely ignore a group of people who have done nothing but kind things for you. Does this make you less good? If so, how do you justify your rude and/or offensive behavior to yourself?

Suppose you think of yourself as kind and caring, but you don't do all the favors people ask of you. As a result, you're riddled with guilt, but should you be?

Every human being struggles with these conflicts. The variations of good behavior and poor behavior seem endless, and these issues make for excellent fiction.

Luckily, epic fantasies make it much more obvious who is good and who is evil. And still, the characters must struggle with their ethical choices for the books to be truly good reads. Simon tells Clary that people are born with the ability to be either good or bad. It's how we conduct ourselves during life that matters. The reader knows that both Simon and Clary struggle— just like real people struggle—with ethical issues, that they must make choices about their behavior. Simon is shown to be extraordinarily kind when he also comments that Hodge didn't have any good role models growing up, which might be why

Valentine's influence over Hodge was so strong. Do you see how Cassandra Clare shows us the theme, as well as Simon's character, in this dialogue? She doesn't simply write, "Simon is a good person." She dramatizes her themes.

Clary and Jace struggle with ethics constantly—an obvious case in point is their romantic love for each other when they still think they're sister and brother. Will struggles constantly too, but for a different reason. Will thinks he's bad because he blames himself for Jem's drug addiction and imminent death. Will keeps trying to be a better person, to be good.

As with many epic fantasies, good versus evil is a huge component of The Mortal Instruments. We're told toward the end of *City of Lost Souls* that basically the world is about to enter total darkness, so dark that light doesn't really exist, so dark that death comes without reason. An epic battle between good and evil is imminent. Simon, an ethical character, struggles to save Jace and to help the cause of good, but as Magnus tells him, "You can't save the world."

WORK TOGETHER FOR THE COMMON GOOD

If ever there was a series of novels that promoted the idea of teamwork, this is it. All of these characters must put aside their issues and disputes, join forces, and work for the common good. When you're faced with an army of demons, what else can you do? When the survival of "every living creature in the world" is at risk (*City of Ashes*, page 264), it's clearly time to sing "Kumbaya" and get on with it. This is basically what Clary's telling everybody when she says that the Downworlders and Shadowhunters have to set aside their petty differences already and work together to fight the demons. The author tosses in subtle references to this theme, as well, by telling us that Shadowhunters believe in multiple truths and the validity of multiple myths. This can be interpreted as indicating that all people are one.

LOVE IS A DOUBLE-EDGED SWORD

Love is hard work. And even when you love someone with all your heart and soul, it can cause great misery. Why? Because if you're a character like Clary or Jace, nasty villains can use your love to twist your mind and make you do things you wouldn't otherwise do. An example is Will's fear of getting near Tessa. He loves her, but God forbid he get anywhere near her because he thinks he's cursed and anyone to whom he gets close will die. This is a good case of forbidden love, as is the forbidden love between Clary and Jace, where Jace avoids Clary because he thinks they're siblings. Cassandra Clare comes up with amazing examples of forbidden love, otherwise known as love is a double-edged sword.

WOMEN'S LIB

Another major theme in these books is that women should be treated more fairly, otherwise known as Come on, Boys, Liberate the Girls Already. Some people call this idea Women's Lib.

One thing you probably noticed is that most of the theme about women's liberation is in the prequel series, The Infernal Devices. This is probably because the prequel takes place in the late 1880s, back when women had very few rights in western societies. The Mortal Instruments is more modern, and so the women enjoy more freedom.

For example, it wasn't that long ago that, in our real world, single girls who became pregnant had a shadow over them. It was considered shameful. We've come a long way—at least in our society—and now, most girls who become pregnant without marriage don't bear the shame and stigma attached to girls in this condition only a decade or two ago. Because Aunt Harriet was pregnant with Nate when her fiancé died on the day before their wedding, Tessa's mother raised Nate to spare Harriet the shame of being a whore, or so says Nate. As readers, we sympathize with Aunt Harriet and feel she's been wronged.

Another example from The Infernal Devices is the idea that it's up to the girls to rebuff male advances because men are weak. This is another old-fashioned idea that was prevalent not so long ago in our own society. In *Clockwork Prince*, Jem tells Tessa that mundane girls are taught that they shouldn't tempt men.

I admit to being disturbed that Maia Roberts gives up her dream of attending Stanford University after Jordan Kyle turns her into a werewolf. But he's a pretty cool guy and actually offers to pay her tuition now that they've found each other again. I'm also disturbed that Clary leaves school, which seems to happen quite a bit in young adult novels. Bella in Twilight didn't go to college. Instead, she just wanted to be with Edward, and she had a child. In the case of Clary, it's understandable because someone attending high school every day can't really battle demons and save the world at the same time. Hence, we assume that all heroes and heroines obtain world-class educations at the Institute. Although we never see her studying . . . and according to Jessamine in The Infernal Devices, girls shouldn't even read novels.

The lack of public education is true for the heroes, too, so it's not quite in the category of Women's Lib. Instead, we have equal opportunity when it comes to dropping out of school.

But let's turn to The Infernal Devices. Here's another example of discrimination against women as we had in our society not that long ago. As a chauvinist, Benedict Lightwood claims that women are ruled by their hearts and have no logic. That line's straight out of the 1960s or even the early '70s.

But it's mainly through Tessa that we feel the difficulties of girls and women in her time. Quite often, she identifies with and remembers Queen Boadicea's strength, and this makes Tessa much stronger.

15

REAL OR NOT REAL?

HERE'S HOW YOU PLAY

This section presents the ground rules of building 3-D characters as opposed to flatter 2-D characters. The objective of the game is to figure out which characters in The Mortal Instruments and The Infernal Devices feel real—that is, 3-D—and which ones do not . . . and why. What does each character want? Do they initiate actions or just follow along like mules? How do they react to other characters' actions and dialogue? Do they have defining appearances, gestures, ways of talking? How does Cassandra Clare make readers love or hate these characters? What's the magic?

The rest of the chapter analyzes some of the characters as defined above. You, as the reader, get to decide whether characters are fully fleshed or 2-D, and why.

If you've ever wanted to follow in Cassandra Clare's footsteps, write fiction, and possibly create something as epic as The Mortal Instruments, these "games" could be very helpful. Even if you aren't interested in writing your own fiction but want to learn more about how Cassandra Clare built her world, I hope these games will provide you with thought-provoking analyses of your favorite characters.

CLARY

What is Clary's initial personality, and why does she behave as she does in the beginning of the series? Would you say that she's strong, intelligent, brave, self-confident, and in control? Think about her role at the Pandemonium Club at the beginning of *City of Bones.* She's resourceful here, as well as intelligent and brave. But she has issues with her self-confidence, thinking of her mother as much prettier and more elegant, and herself as clumsy and rather ordinary in comparison.

She displays her strength, intelligence, and bravery when she battles her first demon, and at first what she wants to do is find her mother. A fully drawn 3-D character will initiate actions to find her mother rather than wait for other characters to do it for her. By the time we're into the middle sections of *City of Bones,* Clary is self-confident and in control of what's she doing. She actually says on page 272, "I know what I'm doing," and then orders Jace to haul Raphael to his feet. This shows the reader Clary's character.

What else do we know about Clary's personality? She's a good friend to Simon, treating him kindly, for example when she keeps trying to save him when he's a rat. She develops her talent and gift of creating runes until she can create new forms that nobody has seen before, showing that she has great perseverance and strength of character. Worried that she *won't* be able to help, striving to do so no matter what it takes, she even makes a Fearless Rune for Jace. It's not easy for her to do so, and she's afraid that she won't be able to do it. Not only does this scene show her bravery and burgeoning skills, it also shows Jace's trust in her and his respect for her abilities.

Her love for Jace strongly affects her and compels her to do things she probably wouldn't have considered years ago. Because of this love, she strikes a bargain with the Queen of Faeries and, rather than request something related to destroying Valentine and the demons, she asks the queen to help her find Jace. She's brave enough to enter an unknown interdimensional pocket of space to try to save him. And her love is so strong that her one request of the Angel Raziel is to bring Jace back to life. Similarly, although she remains upset with her mother about the memory block, she still loves her.

So from the beginning to the end, she's motivated by good, and over the course of the first five books, she grows stronger, more capable, and more self-confident. She wants far more than simply to save her mother. She also wants to save Jace and be with him and, indeed, she wants to save the world. That's a pretty big leap from the Clary we meet at the beginning of *City of Bones.*

If Clary has any defining way of talking in dialogue, it might be that she sometimes sounds much older than her years. She often talks as if she's thirty years old, dispensing great wisdom to the society's leaders.

For a character to be fully developed, she should change over the course of the novel or series of novels. She need not become dramatically different. Above all, writers say that the character should "grow" because real people grow over time. We change, we learn, we evolve. A character who remains the same throughout a novel or series of novels is two-dimensional, flat, unchanging. Real characters, like real people, need flaws because nobody's perfect, and as the story progresses, fully drawn heroines learn to handle these flaws and become better people.

In an interview with Cheryl Brody in *Seventeen* magazine, Cassandra Clare notes that "Clary is certainly flawed—she gets scared, sometimes she makes bad decisions, and she's very stubborn . . . I hope the fact that Clary is a smart, strong girl who faces down her fears will make readers think, *She gets scared just like I would, but she still fights for what she believes in.*"[1]

JACE

Now ask yourself the same questions about Jace. What is he like in the beginning, and does he "grow" over the course of the series? Does he initiate actions that propel the story line forward, or does he follow what others do, acting passively? What motivates him?

We know right away that he's sexy, that he's killed more demons than any other Shadowhunter, that he's cocky, brave, strong, and intelligent. We know all of this about Jace early on. We see these attributes through Isabelle's eyes, which is another way—other than action—to show rather than tell readers about a character. We also know that he's vulnerable, at least to Clary's love. What motivates Jace for a very long time is the desire to do what is right by Clary. He loves her enough to stay away from her, thinking himself dangerous to her well-being.

(Oh, and lest we ever forget, because he thinks they're brother and sister.)

When he becomes Sebastian's "twin" after Lilith's ritual, he changes into a character who is flatlined of feelings. But when that spell breaks, he returns to himself, full of love for Clary and full of good. Perhaps his defining type of dialogue is cocky, unlike Clary, who comes across sounding like someone much older from time to time. His defining appearance might be "golden." While Jace feels a natural jealousy of Simon's friendship with Clary, he saves Simon repeatedly, showing that he's a decent, kind guy. He knows that Alec is in love with him, but he doesn't do anything to make Alec feel uncomfortable about it. He just accepts it as part of their relationship for a long time. Eventually, he opens up and talks to Alec about love. I think that Jace is as three-dimensional as Clary.

SIMON LEWIS

Simon definitely evolves over the course of the novels. He's drawn as somewhat wimpy and nerdy at the beginning of *City of Bones,* but once he gets into the groove as a Daylighter vampire, Simon gains enormous self-confidence, becomes quite brave, and is always selfless. I do think it's a bit odd that Simon continues to profess his undying love for Clary no matter how many times she basically rejects him. He hangs on to that notion for far too long to feel real. That they remain good friends is inspiring.

When asked which character is her favorite, Cassandra Clare answers that it's probably Simon becaue he reminds her of herself. Also, she points out that Simon is the poster boy for why mundanes need to be protected from knowing about the magic realms: It's too dangerous for them. All writers wish we could save our favorite characters from death in our fictional works. Over time, we become very fond of certain characters, and it's hard to say good-bye to them when the story ends—or if the plot dictates that the character must die. In Simon's case, one way to keep him around as a character was to turn him into a vampire, so this is what the author did, though she admits it made her sad to do it.[2]

ISABELLE LIGHTWOOD

Isabelle is also three-dimensional and nicely drawn. Think about it. She starts off being rather nasty, arrogant, and snotty. She's a badass fighter, and she dates boys her parents wouldn't like at all. She ends up being a good friend to Clary, eventually admitting that she needs to do something purposeful and significant. But she's still a badass fighter. As Dani Colvin writes in the *Sunday Tasmanian* in Australia, "And in *City of Lost Souls,* we get to see more of Clare's extraordinary gift for character development; the feisty Isabelle finds herself falling for slightly geeky vampire Simon, while dealing with the loss of a second beloved brother."[3]

ALEC LIGHTWOOD

Alec's main evolution as a character is from "gay guy in the closet" to "gay lover of Magnus" to "so jealous and worried that Magnus is immortal that he attempts to ensure that Magnus becomes mortal and lose his life." I think that's the basic road map. Alec comes across as rather tragic, and he goes from someone who feels like a positive character to someone who feels soft, malleable, and ready to do the wrong thing if it suits his own purposes. He ends up feeling rather self-absorbed. Three-dimensional? I think so, yes.

RAPHAEL SANTIAGO

What do you think about this character, two-dimensional or fully developed? Remember, he must evolve as a character, grow and change over time, and this doesn't mean that he changes to want to rule the vampire universe. Rather, it means the character must change *internally*. In addition, he must have motivations beyond pure evil or pure good. He must learn about himself over time, reflect upon how he might become a different person, and then act on those reflections. I see Raphael as two-dimensional, a holograph projection that shows up every now and then, the hollow three dimensions of the projection almost symbolizing the hollowness of his character. This isn't to say he's not a good character. Novels typically have these types of characters in them as well as fully developed characters. Does anyone else think it's odd that Raphael quite often shows up as a holograph, yet the other characters always appear onstage as solid people? Why don't more people float around in holograph form?

LUKE GARROWAY

Luke grated on my nerves, but then I always have this reaction to what I think of as the Goody Two-shoes characters. In Luke's case, he acts as a stand-in husband to Jocelyn for a crazy number of years, and also serves as a pseudofather figure and mentor to Clary. He's just too good to be true, in my opinion. He has no dimension. For a fictional character to feel real—at least to me—he must have faults as well as positive personality traits. Maybe I'm missing something here. Does Luke have any serious flaws? Does he evolve as a character? I feel as if I'm *supposed* to like him, but I just can't get there.

VALENTINE

Does he evolve over time, or is he always evil? This one's easy. Is Valentine a two-dimensional character or a three-dimensional character? Consider:

He wants his own glorification.

He wants to take over the world.

He wants to kill everybody.

He experiments on pregnant women and babies.

He kills the Silent Brothers. Oh, come on, Valentine, even for *you,* that's really low!

Oh, and I almost forgot, he starves and imprisons angels, too.

I love the bad guys in books. *Love* 'em. They're so over-the-top hilarious. And I love Valentine as a character of evil. They don't get much worse than Valentine. Not even Darth Vader could out-evil this guy. So I like the character, but do I think he's a fully rounded, three-dimensional character? Ummm . . . no.

And that's okay.

SEBASTIAN

On page 134 of *City of Glass,* Cassandra Clare writes that Jace is "all golden" while Sebastian Verlac is "all pallor and shadows." This is about as blatant a description of good versus evil as I can imagine. But Jace is a fully drawn character. What about Sebastian?

He wants to bring Lilith back into the world from interdimensional space.

He wants to be the evil version of Jonathan Shadowhunter.

He wants to marry Clary . . . um, it's the infamous brother-sister issue again, isn't it?

He wants to create a new race of evil Shadowhunters, bound by no laws.

Does this guy have any redeeming features? Does he help orphans? No. Give money to charities? No. Help little old ladies cross the street? No. Want to kill everybody? Yes.

As with Valentine, I like the character of Sebastian Verlac. I wouldn't say he's as developed fictionally as, say, Jace or Will, but he's a lot of fun to read. But then, you see, I have this thing about the bad guys in novels. They're just

too
much
fun!

WILLIAM HERONDALE

I'm going to let you figure out this one. Read my brief analyses of Jace, Simon, Clary, Luke, Valentine, and Sebastian, then determine on your own whether Will is a fully developed character and why. I think he's very well drawn and developed, and he's one of my favorite characters in both The Mortal Instruments and The Infernal Devices. I'm rooting for Will to win Tessa, because like Jace and Clary, these two represent forbidden love, and who wants to deny true love in this bleak world?

JEM (JAMES CARSTAIRS)

He's featured on the cover of *The Infernal Devices: Clockwork Angel* manga (text by Cassandra Clare, art by HyeKyung Baek, Yen Press/Hachette Book Group, 2010). At the end of *Clockwork Prince,* he's the one Tessa chooses as a husband. He's obviously a major character in the prequel series. He's tragic and sympathetic, for who could possibly not feel bad for this nice guy who's addicted to a deadly drug through no real fault of his own? He's a victim. He's sweet. He plays the violin.

Do I like him?

I'm not going to tell you.

Oh, okay, yes yes yes, I do like Jem. However, I like Will more than I like Jem. Will is a much more romantic figure and comes with his own sad and tragic history. Here we go again: Team Will versus Team Jem.

Is Jem a three-dimensional character? Yes, though the strokes of the brush are wide. He certainly has reasons for everything he does, though I'd like to see him change and grow more as a person.

NATE

Think about Nate, the brother who isn't a brother. The Dark Sisters threaten to torture Nate, and Tessa can't bear to think of her brother being tortured, so she endures imprisonment and great torture herself. Tessa's parents died when she was only three, and she's always thought Nate was her real brother. But he's not a good person, is he? He plots against her, he lies about their family and their relationship, he's on the side of Mortmain, oh, and if that were not enough, he killed his own mother, Harriet.

Not a nice fellow, not at all. But is he fully drawn and does he feel like a real person to you? Does he have believable reasons, or motivations, for his actions? I was giving up hope on Nate until the end of *Clockwork Prince*, when he finally shows a tiny drop of humanity and warns Tessa to always wear her angel pendant. So he does evolve from evil to a drop of good.

MORTMAIN

This one's easy. Is he flat as a character; that is, does his character remain static throughout the novels? Does he change from a nice guy into a killer? Or has he always been greedy and despicable? Well, there's your answer. Flat as cardboard, but oh, these bad guys, they are crazy fun to read. He's not as much fun as Valentine or Sebastian, in my opinion, but he does serve his purpose, and as mentioned, not all characters in a book need to be three-dimensional. Most books have large supporting casts.

MRS. DARK AND MRS. BLACK

I couldn't resist tossing in the Dark Sisters, who happen to live in the Dark House. Do you really care if these two are two-dimensional twins of evil? They start out evil. They end up evil. They don't turn bad because somebody close to them twisted their minds at a tender age. They have no real excuse. Cassandra Clare shows us her pulp-love side with these characters, and I love 'em, too. I'm a comic book reader from way back, and I enjoy a pulp story as much as anyone. Mrs. Dark and Mrs. Black could be straight out of a comic book. These are not fully developed characters, but you know something? If they were developed as rational, logical, evolving characters, they wouldn't be nearly as much fun. They make a lot more sense just the way they are. Kudos to Cassandra Clare. I can't say enough good things about these books. They're awesome on so many levels!

16

OPENING CONFLICTS

This chapter briefly analyzes the various plots and how they develop in The Mortal Instruments and The Infernal Devices. It invites you to answer a few questions and to try your own hand at doing what Cassandra Clare has done in your favorite books.

Conflict is when things clash, when events don't occur as we plan or expect. In fiction, when characters clash, disagree, or find themselves at odds, the plot evolves due to this conflict. Sometimes, the conflict can be between characters and an entire society, or it can be between characters and their environment.

Each novel in Cassandra Clare's series begins with a conflict, which is one of the best ways to open a work of fiction. The conflict engages the reader's interest right away, and the author knows that she can provide details and insights much later—typically in the middle sections of a book, where the pace can slow before picking up speed again and roaring toward the finale. In the case of The Mortal Instruments and The Infernal Devices, the author maintains her pace throughout the novels with almost no lull. This isn't an easy method, and I think she pulls it off because she has taken very long scenes and spliced them into pieces, then arranged all the pieces into a linear jigsaw puzzle. So we have a scene with, say, Clary and Jace, followed by a scene with Simon, then a scene with Isabelle, then we're back to Clary and Jace, and so forth. This chopping of extended scenes into smaller pieces keeps the suspense and the action moving. And this pace is evident from page one of *City of Bones*.

Let's look at the opening scenes of each novel.

City of Bones opens with Clary and Simon getting into the "all ages" Pandemonium Club on a Sunday. I can't resist noting here that, from what we learn about the Pandemonium Club much later in these books—it's a hangout where supernatural beings take advantage of mundanes with gambling and dark magic, etc.—it's a bit peculiar that the club would be open on Sundays to "all ages," code for children and underaged teens. But let's cast that point aside and take it on faith that a demonic-oriented club would open its doors on Sunday in this way, and return to Clary and Simon as they enter the club.

The conflict immediately arises when the author switches the *point of view* from Clary to an unknown boy wearing glamours. By point of view, I mean that we see the unfolding events, the actions, and we directly know the thoughts of a particular character, in this case, a boy who is actually a demon.

By the second page, we already know—without any doubt—

that the book is a fantasy with supernatural elements. For one thing, the boy thinks about the glamours on his blade and his eyes, both of which fool the mundanes into thinking he's an ordinary boy. The glamours basically hide the paranormal beings, help them fade into their surroundings, and glamours can even make entire buildings invisible.

By the third page, we know that the boy is going to give Clary and Simon trouble in the form of some serious conflict. He's nearly fainting from the essence of the ordinary humans, or mundanes, around him in the club. He thinks about trying to survive in his own "dead world" and how easy it would be for the mundanes to die. As he considers how delicious it will be when the girl dies, we're ready for Clary and Simon to swing into action and save her. We already know from the action of this demonic character that Clary and Simon will be on the side of good.

Does this scene evoke an emotional response from you? Most likely, it does! Are you frightened for the girl? Do you think the demonic boy is dreadful and should be thwarted? Most likely, you're drawn into *City of Bones* and can't put it down . . . as soon as you read the first couple of pages.

How does Cassandra Clare do it? *Action, conflict, characterization.*

Now go back and read the closing paragraphs of chapter 1 in *City of Bones*. What do you know about Clary and Simon at this point? You probably care about them as characters. You may think of Simon as the responsible, adultlike one of the two friends. You may have guessed that The Mortal Instruments is mainly Clary's story, although there will be many other points of view. You probably realize that this will be an epic fantasy story, that you will encounter demons from other dimensions, warlocks, vampires, and other supernaturals; that Clary will fall in love, that Simon will be in love with her and want her, that she'll be torn between Simon and the character with whom she ends up falling in love. In fact, you probably know that this character will be Jace, simply from the dialogue and actions in the first chapter. You know that Clary and Simon live in Brooklyn, that the story will be set in modern times. You will know all of the above by the time you flip the page to chapter 2.

Now read the first chapter of *City of Ashes* again. Where does it take place, from whose point of view does it open, and what is the central conflict?

It opens in Manhattan from a *distant point of view*. On page 2, do you know whose head you are inside? Is any specific character feeling great emotion? No. Instead, you feel as if you're standing across the room from these characters, and somebody—the narrator—is telling you their story. How do you know this? Some clues:

"The man standing in front of the window didn't look particularly impressed by" the view, and "there was a frown on his . . . face" (*City of Ashes,* page 2). If the point of view were inside this man's mind, then he could not possibly see the frown on his face. So you know that you're not deep inside his point of view.

The same is true of the boy in this scene: "The membranous black wings protruding from his narrow shoulder blades . . . flapped nervously" (ibid.). As with the man's frown, the boy would not be thinking to himself, Oh, my membranous black wings that protrude from my narrow shoulder blades are flapping nervously. People don't think this way about themselves. So we're either in a very distant point of view of the boy, or the narrator is telling us the story. At this point, for me anyway, it feels as if the narrator rather than a specific character is talking to me. Due to the distance, for me, the conflict isn't as acute as the opening of *City of Bones*.

By page 3, I've figured out the point of view. It's the boy, not the man. How do I know this, and why do we care? I know it because of the sentence, "The man sounded pleased." If inside the man's mind, there's no way he would think about himself, *Oh, I sound pleased.* Directly after this section, we clearly step inside the mind of the boy, Elias, in the paragraph that begins, "Elias got to his feet . . ." And now, the conflict grasps my attention. I'm worried about the man because Elias is a warlock who is using pentagrams and talking in a language called Chthonian, which by the way, could be a nod to H. P. Lovecraft's Cthulhu Mythos. On the other hand, Chthonian may simply refer to the traditional use of the word pertaining to creatures of the underworld. Or both.

As Elias brings forth the demon Agramon, the author has sucked us in again. We can't stop reading. And now I'm worried about Elias instead of the man because Agramon—a fantastically Lovecraftian creature, by the way—crushes the boy like a Lovecraftian ooze. End of Elias, and with him, goes his point of view. Suddenly, we're back to the distant point of view, the story being told by the narrator, who is the author. It's a bit disconcerting, this opening chapter with point of view complexities, but it doesn't matter overall. By the time we're on page 5, the end of chapter 1, Valentine is onstage, and he has the Mortal Cup. We will read on . . .

Think about the conflict in the opening chapter. Elias versus Valentine? Elias versus Valentine and Agramon? Again, we're sucked in by action and conflict, and as for characterization, we have the thrill of Valentine stepping onstage and announcing that he has the Mortal Cup. *Beautiful.*

What is your emotional response, if any, to this opening scene? Are you horrified? Are you thrilled? Do you hate Valentine for killing Elias? Do you feel sorry for Elias, and if so, why?

If you want to write your own fiction—a novel or a series that you hope to publish—you should study how Cassandra

Clare structures her openings. Then you should try to write an opening scene of your own that starts in a specific point of view and introduces an extremely dramatic conflict. Try it and see what happens.

Examine the opening chapter of *City of Glass*, the third book in the series. It's told from Clary's point of view, and she's with Simon again. On page 3, she thinks about saving her mother, and she dreams about being with Jace but their romance is on the skids because he thinks that he's Valentine's son. The point of view switches on page 12 to Simon, and at the very end of the chapter, Jace and Simon discover the dead Madeleine.

Is this opening chapter as strong as in the first two books? Why, or why not? Is the conflict slower, more drawn out? Does the author supply backfill, that is, does she tell us a few things we need to know that already happened in the first two books? What is your emotional response to this opening chapter? I'll leave you on your own to study the opening chapters of *City of Fallen Angels* and *City of Lost Souls*. Take them apart, identify the opening conflict and the opening point of view characters. How does the author end these opening chapters, with a cliffhanger, with an emotional pull on her readers?

If you want to explore additional intricacies, study the opening chapters of *Clockwork Angel* and *Clockwork Prince*, the prequels. You don't need more action to draw you into a story than the opening sentence on page 1 of *Clockwork Angel*, "The demon exploded in a shower of ichor and guts." The point of view character is William Herondale, and we know that his friend's name is Jem, and that Will is going to be a hero in this series because he's already worried about Jem's safety. We know that it's set in London in 1878, that Shadowhunters will be featured, as well as demons, glamours, and other trappings of The Mortal Instruments. We know on page 5 that the story will involve alchemy and the ouruboros. And then by page 6, we're deeply into Tessa's point of view and the world of steampunk. The chapter closes with conflict, as the Dark Sisters show up and cart Tessa off. The conflicts are Will and Jem versus demons and then Tessa being sucked into the world of the Dark Sisters. The points of view, Will and then Tessa, tip us off that these will be two of the major characters in this series. By the end of the first chapter, the reader fears for Tessa at the hands of the creepy sisters, and I don't know about you, but I definitely figured that Tessa and Will would become romantically involved in some way and that Jem would form the third point of the romantic triangle.

Let's shift now to some of the main quest plots in these novels; as with the number of characters, there are quite a few adventures in these books. A *quest plot* basically involves a character or group of characters who seek something or someone, and it drives the motivation of the characters, which, in turn, propels the story forward.

17

SEARCHING FOR SOMETHING

SELF-IDENTITY QUESTS

Who's human, who's part human, do the major characters even know who their parents are? What's the true purpose and meaning of these characters' lives?

At minimum, Clary, Tessa, and Jace are all trying to discover the identity of their parents, the nature of their very selves (mundane versus Shadowhunter versus demon versus warlock, mixtures of various types of creatures with various types of powers, etc.), and the meaning of their lives. Along with the romantic plots, the identity quests are key to these books.

Early in *City of Bones*, Clary already wonders about the

nature of her mother. Does she really *know* her mother? She doesn't think so. The factor that immediately tips off the reader that Clary is going to be baffled about her own identity and destiny. Later, she realizes that she's a Shadowhunter and finds out about the nature of her real father. This sends her reeling into another world, a magical one she hadn't known existed. It forever alters the course of her life. Because she discovers who and what she really is, she ends up leaving her "mundane" high school and life, and she winds up leading a crusade against pure supernatural evil. We know she's going to be someone even more special by the end of *City of Lost Souls,* as she saves Jace, not only her love but also a special new form of angelic being. Her identity quest isn't quite yet over, any more than Jace knows what he really is by the end of the fifth book.

On page 62 of *City of Fallen Angels,* Jace reads letters to learn about his real family. Like Clary, Jace is baffled about his roots and where he comes from and what he is and why. The Queen of Faeries tells Jace to ask Valentine "what blood runs in his veins" (*City of Ashes,* page 167). We puzzle endlessly, it seems, about the identity of his father. First we think his father might have been Michael Wayland, who died in a car accident. Or maybe, his father was the evil Valentine, and maybe this makes Clary his sister. Could it be? Without this identity quest, the entire romantic problem of brother-sister would fall apart, flattening much of the emotional rush of the books. Or maybe his father was really Stephen Herondale, and that would solve the brother-sister problem, at long last. Now try to puzzle through the wrinkles of the Herondale family. Oh, my goodness, and good luck with that! Here's how I figure it (and I may be wrong, who knows?): Inquisitor Imogen Herondale had a son named Stephen Herondale, who married Amatis but then divorced her when Valentine wanted him to marry somebody else. So Stephen married Celine, who killed herself . . . but by the way, she apparently is Jace's real mother. It's no wonder Jace can't figure out where he comes from and who is family really is . . . But there's more to the puzzle, of course. Imogen Herondale's husband, Marcus, died of heartbreak, and I think this makes Marcus the . . . excuse me while I scratch my head . . . grandfather of Jace.

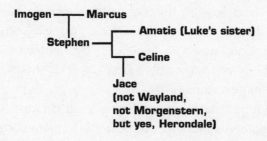

But oh no, how do we puzzle William Herondale into this picture of Jace's ancestry?

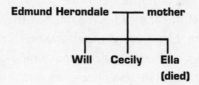

I'm not sure where Will Herondale fits into Jace's family tree. Was he Marcus Herondale's father or grandfather? Was he an uncle or brother of Marcus? All of this requires a much smarter mind than mine. All I know is that William Herondale is related to Jace Herondale, that William should be Tessa's one true love (in my opinion!), and that Jace is Clary's one true love.

While it may seem as if Jace's identity quest centers primarily around his parents, there's far more to it than his Shadowhunter past. The entire meaning of his life changes when he transforms into a new angelic form. He's not just the world's best demon killer, he's now the *hope* of the entire world. We get the feeling that he and Clary might become a true couple, that their offspring may become an entirely new race of creatures, those who can finally defeat demonic evil, once and for all. We don't know this, of course, not yet—not until the author concludes the series and possibly another series to come, one that tells us the stories of this new race. I'm only guessing what might come, but I do know that Jace doesn't yet know exactly who or what he is yet, not at the end of *City of Lost Souls.* There's definitely more to come.

Speaking of Clary, her past isn't quite as complex. We know that her mother is Jocelyn Fray, who was formerly Jocelyn Fairchild. Supposedly, her father was Jonathan Clark, or so we're led to believe, but later we learn that her father was really Valentine. Here, my emotional reaction is mainly to feel horrible for Clary that her father is Valentine. I also think her mother must have been insane to have a child with Valentine, and I don't really care if he seemed nice back then. I mean, come on, he's like Darth Vader with a sickening veneer of charm! As an aside, it's amusing that Valentine's last name is Morgenstern rather than something supermacho like Strongarm. The author clearly has a fun sense of humor.

But poor Tessa has the identity quest from hell! Her brother, Nate, really isn't her brother. Her father is supposedly Richard Gray, and she's an orphan. On pages 51–52 of *Clockwork Angel,* she's already having nightmares and wondering who and what she is, literally. Later, Brother Enoch's voice tells her that she's an Eidolon, or shape-changer, but that she bears no demon mark. Charlotte tells her that she's a Downworlder, which we take to mean a vampire, werewolf, faerie, or warlock, but no-body seems to know what *kind* of Downworlder she is. It could be that Tessa is something new, a type of creature the world has not yet seen.

The ultimate identity quest from hell, of course, is that Tessa can Change into anyone, and hence she may not actually be any one person. As she wonders on page 111 of *Clockwork Angel,* "When she Changed back into herself, how was she to know there wasn't some slight shift in her very self, something that made her not who she was anymore?" and "Was her face nothing but a mask of flesh, irrelevant to her true self?" (ibid.).

Is she a warlock? A demon? A human? Everybody's debating what she is, and she thinks about it a lot. It speaks to her strength of character that her identity quest from hell doesn't make her go mad or crumple her into a drug or drink-addled mess. She holds it together pretty well, even in light of Mort-main's horrific declaration that Tessa isn't really any single person. The reader wonders if it's possible that a future book in the series will unveil that Tessa is everybody yet nobody, that per-haps she carries a thousand identities. And yet she does have an individual personality and character, she has a soul—as the books tell us—and we clearly perceive her as a distinct entity, a character unto herself. As with Jace at the end of *City of Lost Souls,* Tessa by the end of *Clockwork Prince* doesn't quite know what she will be and what it means. We do know that her life depends on this knowledge, that forces are trying to control and conquer her simply because she's something unique. The meaning of our lives, those of us who are mundanes in the real world, spins around our families, our friends, and what we do for both our vocations and our avocations. The meaning of Tessa's life differs in that it spins around *what she is* far more than whether she decides to become a seamstress or a muffin maker in steampunk England. I remain fascinated by Tessa Gray as one of my very favorite characters in this series.

TREASURE QUESTS

Are the main characters looking for objects of any kind in The Mortal Instruments and The Infernal Devices? One major treasure quest is that the characters must find the Mortal Instruments. Some minor treasure quests involve Clary seeking the set of faerie rings for the Queen of the Seelie Court. After finding the rings, Clary is able to communicate with Simon via mental telepathy, enabling her to look for Jace in an unknown dimensional pocket without the minor quest, the major treasure quest would be much more challenging.

CHASING MORTMAIN

In this case, a major quest is for a person, Mortmain, rather than for identity, objects, or treasure. For a long time, Tessa, Will, and Jem don't know who the Magister really is, and toward the end of the first Infernal Devices book, they have to find him.

18

DISHING UP
THE DIRT

Every reader—and good author—knows how important it is to provide information about the characters and events of previous books in a series. Otherwise, readers may get lost, not remember what happened in, say, book 2, while they're reading book 4. Authors have a bunch of tricks up their sleeves to take care of this problem. One method is through flashbacks, whereby a character remembers what happened previously. Another method is through an infodump, or backfill, in which the author just dumps background information on the page to provide readers with facts about characters and events.

Both flashbacks and infodumps distance the reader from the actual story line. We're taken back in time, we jump from the here and now of the story, and then must return to the on-stage action when the flashback or infodump ends.

For a flashback, the author should provide a smooth transition from onstage story time into a character's memory of what's already transpired. Because The Mortal Instruments and The Infernal Devices move very quickly, with the action exploding constantly across the pages via carefully done scene splices and interruptions of characters as they supply key information, flashbacks aren't central to these books. These aren't slow-moving stories with people mooning over the past and weeping by shimmering lakes while remembering lost ones and difficult times.

Infodumps are another matter. There are a lot of them in these books, which isn't to say they don't work well within the context of the story. Sometimes, in a novel that's this packed with action, the reader welcomes a short period in which things slow down.

An infodump is typically supplied via narrative blocks, or exposition, or via dialogue between two characters. Basically, an infodump explains more about the characters, who they are and where they came from, and it also tells readers why there are problems in the world of the story. It's easy to have one character tell another about all sorts of things that have happened in the past. It provides key information about previous events without putting the events onstage in the actual story line.

Infodumps should be applied in small doses. Otherwise, it's obvious to the reader that the author is dumping information on the page, and it can jerk us out of the story that's onstage.

Flip to pages 273–275 of *City of Glass* and start reading where Hodge says, "I knew he would return someday. I knew he would make a bid for power again," and so on. Through dialogue with Clary and Jace, we learn a lot of backfill information about Hodge and Valentine. We discover Hodge's motivation as a character, that he wanted freedom from his curse. He continues on page 274 at length, ignoring Clary's request that they return to action, as he explains that he was locked in the Institute for fifteen years, doing a lot of research, and then on the next page, he tells Clary and Jace what he learned through that research.

Do you think the description on pages 273–275 is too lengthy? Does it distance you from the main action? Or is the length suitable?

This description was fine with me, it didn't jerk me out of the story at all, and it provided just the right amount of information.

Another nicely written example is on pages 10–11 of *City of Lost Souls.* Here, Clary tells the reader via flashback about things that have transpired after the end of *City of Fallen Angels.* In one long paragraph, we learn about the Council's trial and what it ruled about Clary's fate. How do you know that this is a flashback? Look for the clue. Can you find it? On page 10, Clary thinks that "she couldn't help but remember . . . ," and then she does indeed remember what happened. This is a phrase that was used constantly on the long-running television show *Sex and the City,* and it's a phrase that I notice often now in other film and TV shows as well as stories and books. After the flashback, the memory of her trial, the next paragraph begins with, "Clary sighed and flipped her phone open to check the time." This sentence pulls the reader back into the time of the current story. Smoothly done, isn't it?

Now flip to page 120 of *City of Lost Souls* and look for the one-paragraph infodump from Clary's point of view. Like the two previous examples, this one is also short, swift, and nicely drawn. The tip-off that it's an infodump is the opening sentence, beginning with, "The Iron Sisters, Clary knew, were [etc.,

etc.].″ The author could just as easily used the phrase "couldn't help but remember," as in, "The Iron Sisters, Clary couldn't help but remember, were [etc., etc.]." But she chooses something different and slips the memory in so smoothly we barely notice it happening.

Now let's look at a much longer infodump on pages 206–207 of *City of Fallen Angels*. Does this one work, or is it too long for you? Jordan is telling Simon about his past, about Maia, about what happened between the two of them long ago. Notice how the author splices Jordan's retelling of past events with tiny action from the current story time. For example, after talking at length, Jordan pauses for a moment—"His voice trailed off." And then Jordan sips some coffee, and to skewer us directly into current story time, the author expertly adds, from Simon's point of view, that Jordan looks sick. And then we return to the infodump. Again, this is very smoothly written. If you read the rest of the material on page 207, you'll find other examples of how Cassandra Clare breaks up Jordan's memories and adds jots of action from the current story time.

I did find the repetitions of backfill about Shadowhunters, Downworlders, the Angel Raziel, the Mortal Cup, and so forth, a tad overdone. We learn very early—on pages 78–79 of *City of Bones*—the origin story of the Shadowhunters, that they're called Nephilim, about the Circle, and so forth. But then there's an incredibly long stretch later in the book, on pages 390–402, that gives us backfill information about all of this, and more. Basically, this later section sums up all sorts of important information we need to know before continuing in the series. The origin story is repeated again on pages 43–44 of *City of Glass,* in case we forgot it from the first two books. The prequel series also supplies the same backfill, as on pages 98–99 and later on page 370 of *Clockwork Angel.*

If these repetitions bother you, keep in mind that not everybody reads all of these books one after the other. Many people read a book, then wait six months before tackling the next one. So it does help to have repetition of the origin story from book to book. Within the same book, however, it helps to keep such repetitions of information to a minimum.

Also, I don't have to tell you that this entire series is incredibly complex: many dozens of characters, many types of supernatural beings, many intricacies, and so repeating key information is actually useful when we are trying to keep things straight. I read the first seven books of this series twice, and the world is so elaborate, real, and intricate that it does help to refresh my memory from time to time.

19

MINI-BIOGRAPHY OF CASSANDRA CLARE

assandra Clare was born Judith A. Rumelt on July 31, 1973, in Tehran, Iran, and now lives in Amherst, Massachusetts, with her husband and three cats.[1] Her parents were teaching in Tehran when she was born.

Her grandfather was Max Rosenberg, who produced about seventy-five films, most of them involving supernatural, horror, or science-fiction elements. One of his films, *The Curse of Frankenstein,* starring Peter Cushing, made $7 million.[2] He was also behind *Tales From the Crypt* and *At the Earth's Core.* Rosenberg was born in 1914 in the Bronx in New York City. His wife was Isabele W. Rosenberg, and after she died, he endowed a special weekly story hour for children in her name in Jerusalem. We can't help but wonder if Cassandra Clare named a character Isabelle in honor of her grandmother.

Rosenberg's daughter, social worker Elizabeth Rosenberg Rumelt, is Cassandra Clare's mother, and her father is Richard Rumelt, born in 1942 in Washington, D.C. He's the author of various academic business books, such as *Good Strategy/Bad Strategy: The Difference and Why It Matters.* He earned his BS and MS in engineering from the University of California at Berkeley, worked as a system engineer at the Jet Propulsion Laboratory, and was instrumental in founding the Iran Center for Management Studies.[3] Cassandra Clare acknowledges the strong influence of her father on her career, noting that he instilled in her the idea that writers need to have marketing plans and strategies to sell their work and manage their own careers.[4]

Starting as a reporter for entertainment magazines and tabloid newspapers, including the *National Enquirer* and the *Star,* by 2007, she achieved the honor of finalist for the Locus Award for Best First Novel for *City of Bones* and went on to great fame and regard as author of the highly acclaimed The Mortal Instruments and The Infernal Devices series.

Cassandra Clare is her pen name, and she wrote Harry Potter and The Lord of the Rings fan fiction under another very similar pen name, Cassandra Clair.

Her goal in writing fiction is the same as expressed by many authors, including myself. We all want readers to enjoy our books. It really is as simple as that. As she puts it, "My goals for my books is that I hope they are read and enjoyed by many people."[5]

Cassandra Clare moved around the world throughout childhood, and by her first years in elementary school, she had already lived in several foreign countries, including England, Switzerland, and France. She even spent a month as a toddler in her father's backpack as he hiked with her mother in the Himalaya Mountains.[6]

In an interview with Cynthia Leitich Smith on the Cynsations Web site, Cassandra Clare says that when she was a teenager, she was "really quiet, which is always a shocker for people who know me now."[7] As with many of us who read constantly, books became good friends to her.

And, as with many of us who are authors, her love of reading evolved into writing books.[8]

It is well known that her favorite authors include many classic and famous fantasists such as J. R. R. Tolkien, C. S. Lewis, Madeleine L'Engle, Philip Pullman, and J. K. Rowling.[9] Given that these authors write about groups of children who discover magical objects or pass through portals to enter magical worlds, it's easy to see how much her favorite novels influenced her decision to write The Mortal Instruments series. Sarah Moroz, who interviewed her for *Publishers Weekly,* explains that growing up, "Clare had read hard-boiled detective stories and was a huge fan of '80-era urban fantasy, notably Terri Windling's *Borderland.*"[10] This might explain why her books are action-packed urban fantasies.

When she was thirteen, Cassandra Clare wrote the thousand-page novel, *The Beautiful Cassandra.*[11] We know where she got her pen name! It probably came from long ago, when she wrote *The Beautiful Cassandra.*

Although she moved to Los Angeles, California, where she attended high school, she returned to New York City in the summers to visit her grandparents, who lived on the Upper East Side. She had the good fortune to be in a creative writing class in school while also being exposed to a great deal of New York City, where she would later set The Mortal Instruments.[12]

In a *Powells.com* interview, she says, "I write books for teenagers because when I was a teenager, that was the best reading time of my life. It was the time I experienced reading the most intensely and read the most widely and with the most excitement."[13]

After graduating from college, she went to work as a writer for tabloids and entertainment magazines. Sarah Moroz quotes her as saying that her work for the tabloids prepared her for "the creation of a fictional narrative."[14]

By 2006, she was writing her own fantasy fiction full time. She says—quite famously, for this quote is repeated all over the Internet—that the idea for The Mortal Instruments arose when she was at a tattoo parlor in New York City's East Village.[15]

In *The Straits Times,* Cassandra Clare tells interviewer Andrea Ong that she thinks that readers like urban fantasy novels because they let us daydream about finding the magical and secret world connected to our real one.[16] She also notes that urban fantasy enables her to create strong, modern heroines.

As an adult, she moved permanently to New York in 2001. In an interview in the *New Zealand Herald,* she says, "That was when I started working on the books as I reconnected with my New York roots."[17] She based Clary's home on the apartment she had in Park Slope in Brooklyn, and Luke's home on her first apartment in Williamsburg. As for the Institute, it's on the Upper East Side.

As mentioned, character Isabelle's name may be a tribute to her grandmother, Isabele Rosenberg, but in addition, she tells interviewer Stacey Hayman that her cat, Simon, "stayed with me through six moves and three different cities. I named Simon in TMI [The Mortal Instruments] after him."[18] Given how much she loved her cat, Simon, perhaps Chairman Meow is one of her favorite characters in The Mortal Instruments.

Cassandra Clare doesn't talk much to interviewers about her private life, but she does maintain an extremely active and high-profile visibility on the Internet. Just hop over to her Tumblr page, and you'll find all kinds of great information about her books and the *City of Bones* movie. She posts her thoughts about characters and stories, and she also slips in clues about her upcoming books. Her fan following is enormous and solid. She's friendly and open to readers, so I encourage you to stop by her Web sites and chat with her.

I've written more Companion Guides than I can remember. I've read so many young adult novels that you'd think I was addicted to them. And maybe I am. Sometimes, a series just hits me as remarkable and special, and both The Mortal Instruments and The Infernal Devices are in that category. I didn't read the books because I had to read them for this Companion Guide. I read the books because I really like them. And I'll read the next novels in both series, simply for pleasure. It's been fun talking to you about these books, and if you want to continue the discussion, let's do so. I'll see you on the Internet, and until then,

Keep reading!

Lois H. Gresh
January 14, 2013

Blog: http://loisgresh.blogspot.com
Twitter: @lois_gresh
Goodreads: http://www.goodreads.com/loisgresh

NOTES AND RESOURCES

A book such as this one requires a lot of research. Not only did I read the current seven novels in The Mortal Instruments and The Infernal Devices series twice, I also read an enormous number of other books, as well as newspaper and magazine articles and a few Internet materials, before I started writing *The Mortal Instruments Companion.* What follows are my notes and other reference sources.

1. Which Is the Best Book and Movie of All?

1. David A. Kaplan, "A Most Unusual Father-Daughter Professional Pairing," features.blogs.fortune.cnn.com/2012/08/29/Cassandra-clare-richard-rumelt.
2. Alexandra Alter, "The Weird World of Fan Fiction," *Wall Street Journal,* June 15, 2012, p. D1.

3. Hanna Flint, "Katniss Who? Lily Collins Works Her Magic as the Lead in Teen Fantasy Film *The Mortal Instruments: City of Bones,*" *Daily Mail Online,* December 21, 2012, www.dailymail.co.uk/tvshowbiz/article-2251528/Lily-Collins-works-magic-Jamie-Campbell-Bower-trailer-teen-fantasy-The-Mortal-instrument-City-Of-Bones.html.

4. Breia Brissey, "Cassandra Clare Talks 'Mortal Instruments' Movie and Teases Her Other Series," *Entertainment Weekly,* November 13, 2012, http://shelf-life.ew.com/2012/11/13/cassandra-clare-the-mortal-instruments-movie-city-of-bones/.

5. Breia Brissey, "First Look: Cassandra Clare's 'Mortal Instruments' Movie," *Entertainment Weekly,* November 14, 2012, http://shelf-life.ew.com/2012/11/14/mortal-instruments-movie-first-look-cassandra-clare/.

6. Perez Hilton, "Lily Collins Plays with The Mortal Instruments in FIRST Trailer! WATCH HERE!," November 15, 2012, http://perezhilton.com/category/jamie-campbell-bower#.UPGKcEK5f8s.

7. Paul Scott, "His Three Ex-wives Have Cost Him £42m—No Wonder There's No Fool Like an Old Phil," *Daily Mail Online,* August 22, 2008, www.dailymail.co.uk/tvshowbiz/article-1048373/His-ex-wives-cost-42m–wonder-theres-fool-like-old-Phil.html.

8. www.glamourmagazine.co.uk/celebrity/biographies/lily-collins, www.tvguide.com/celebrities/lily-collins/bio/307030.

9. http://iheartcollins.org/about/biography/.

10. Lauren Brown, "From Her Spice Girls Obsession to Her Signature Eyebrows, Get to Know Hollywood Darling Lily Collins!" August 13, 2012, www.glamour.com/entertainment/blogs/obsessed/2012/08/from-her-spice-girls-obsession.html.

11. www.businessinsider.com/where-celebrity-kids-go-to-school-2012-9?op=1.

12. Alison Schwartz and Kristin Luna, "Lily Collins 'So Excited' to Play Snow White Opposite Julia Roberts," *People,* April 2, 2011, www.people.com/people/article/0,,20478906,00.html.

13. www.kidzworld.com/article/26797-lily-collins-bio.

14. Brissey, "Cassandra Clare Talks 'Mortal Instruments' Movie."

15. http://uk.linkedin.com/pub/david-bower/9/478/a20.

16. www.nymt.org.uk/.

17. Melissa Whitworth, "Fresh Blood: Jamie Campbell Bower's Teen Thrills," *London Evening Standard,* November 12, 2009, www.standard.co.uk/lifestyle/fresh-blood-jamie-campbell-bowers-teen-thrills-6780359.html.

18. Katie Nicholl, "Young Potter Stars Split as the Magic Wears Off," *Daily Mail Online,* July 1, 2012, www.dailymail.co.uk/tvshowbiz/article-2167145/Bonnie-Wright-Jamie-Campbell-Bower-Young-Potter-stars-split-magic-wears-off.html.

19. "Top Acting Talent to Watch in 2013," *Herald Sun* (Melbourne), January 3, 2013, www.heraldsun.com.au/entertainment/movies/top-acting-talent-to-watch-in-2013/story-e6frf9h6-1226546915892.

20. Lesley Savage, "'New Moon' Volturi Member Jamie Campbell Bower Wants More Power," *Entertainment Weekly PopWatch*, November 25, 2009, http://popwatch.ew.com/2009/11/25/new-moon-volturi-member-jamie-campbell-bower-wants-more-power/.

21. Jenn Selby, "Jamie Campbell Bower: BD2 Ending 'Bitter Sweet' for Twilight Fans," *Glamour*, November 16, 2012, www.glamourmagazine.co.uk/celebrity/celebrity-news/2012/11/16/jamie-campbell-bower-bd2-ending-bitter-sweet-twilight.

22. http://cassandraclare.tumblr.com/post/26996750246/casting-news-simon.

23. Natalie C. Markey, "'City of Bones' Has Its Simon—Robert Sheehan," *Examiner*, July 11, 2012, www.examiner.com/article/city-of-bones-has-its-simon.

24. http://cassandraclare.tumblr.com/post/25466999021/casting-news-isabelle.

25. www.telegraph.co.uk/culture/film/starsandstories/9528140/Jemima-West-interview-why-playing-a-prostitute-is-never-black-and-white.html.

26. Annette Bourdeau, "Kevin Zegers on 'Titanic: Blood & Steel' and his Jaunty Mustache," *HuffPost TV*, September 19, 2012, www.huffingtonpost.com/2012/09/19/titanic-blood-steel-kevin-zegers-interview_n_1897615.html.

27. Brissey, "Cassandra Clare Talks 'Mortal Instruments' Movie."

ADDITIONAL RESOURCES

www.tvguide.com/celebrities/lily-collins/bio/307030.

Paul Lester, "Phil Collins: A Groovy Kind of Life," *Express*, www.express.co.uk/posts/view/199003/Phil-Collins-A-groovy-kind-of-life-. See this Web page for a nice photo of Lily Collins with her father, Phil Collins.

2. Spinning a Faerie Good Tale

1. M. M. Hall, "Redefining Paranormal Romance," *Publishers Weekly*, July 16, 2007, p. 149.

2. See Cassandra Clare's emotionally moving Tumblr post about Internet bullies: http://cassandraclare.tumblr.com/post/33442496804/october-is-anti-bullying-month-on-hiatuses-and-hate.

3. Stephen Jewell, "Magical Tales Take on Life of Their Own," *New Zealand Herald*, www.nzherald.co.nz/entertainment/news/article.cfm?c_id=1501119&objectid=10722525.

4. Andrea Ong, "Monsters, Inc; Forget Middle Earth. Demons and Other

Fantasy Creatures Are Now Living in Cities, at Least in Books," *Straits Times* (Singapore), March 26, 2006.

ADDITIONAL RESOURCES

John Thackray Bunce, *Fairy Tales, Their Origin and Meaning: with Some Account of Dwellers in Fairyland* (London: Macmillan, 1878).

Marie-Louise von Franz, *An Introduction to the Psychology of Fairy Tales* (Zurich: Spring Publications, 1970).

Pamela Allardice, *Myths, Gods & Fantasy* (Santa Barbara, CA: ABC-CLIO, 1991).

Susan Sellers, *Myth and Fairy Tale in Contemporary Women's Fiction* (New York: Palgrave, 2001).

3. Romantic Fantasies

RESOURCES

Susan Ostrov Weisser, ed., *Women and Romance: A Reader* (New York: New York University Press, 2001).

Sarah S. G. Frantz and Eric Murphy Selinger, eds., *New Approaches to Popular Romance Fiction: Critical Essays* (Jefferson, NC: McFarland & Company, 2012).

5. Angels and Shadowhunters: The Creation Myth of The Mortal Instruments and The Infernal Devices

1. A. C. Coleridge, ed., "The Belgic Confession of Faith," *Reformed Confessions of the 16th Century* (Philadelphia: Westminster, 1966), p. 196.
2. Geddes MacGregor, *Angels: Ministers of Grace* (New York: Paragon House, 1988).
3. Peter J. Kreeft, *Angels (and Demons): What Do We Really Know About Them?* (San Francisco: Ignatius Press, 1995), p. 7.
4. Michael Shermer, *Why People Believe Weird Things: Pseudoscience, Superstition, and Other Confusions of Our Time* (New York: W. H. Freeman, 1997), p. 10.
5. Paul Tillich, *Theology of Culture* (New York: Oxford University Press, 1959), pp. 4–5.

ADDITIONAL RESOURCES

Peter Marshall and Alexandra Walsham, eds., *Angels in the Early Modern World* (New York: Cambridge University Press, 2006).

Gustav Davidson, *A Dictionary of Angels, Including the Fallen Angels* (New York: Free Press, 1967).

Rosemary Ellen Guiley, *Encyclopedia of Angels* (New York: Facts on File, 1996).

Norma Lorre Goodrich, *Myths of the Hero* (New York: Orion Press, 1962).

Charles H. Long, *Alpha: The Myths of Creation* (New York: George Braziller, 1963).

David Maclagan, *Creation Myths: Man's Introduction to the World* (London: Thames and Hudson, 1977).

8. Big Bad Mother Demon: Lilith, Her Minions, and Possession

1. http://cassandraclare.tumblr.com/post/15992791283/i-was-just-re -reading-cofa-and-i-got-to-the-part-where.
2. John L. Nevius, D.D. *Demon Possession and Allied Themes: Being an Inductive Study of Phenomena of Our Own Times* (Chicago: Fleming H. Revell, 1894), pp. 285–86.

ADDITIONAL RESOURCES

L. J. Elmer, "Demon (Theology of)," *New Catholic Encyclopedia,* 2nd ed., 15 vols. (Detroit: Gale, 2003). 4:646–50.

Manfred Lurker, *Dictionary of Gods and Goddesses, Devils and Demons* (New York: Routledge, 1988).

Karel van der Toorn, Bob Becking, and Peter W. van der Horst, eds., *Dictionary of Deities and Demons in the Bible* (New York: E. J. Brill, 1995).

Stephen Addiss, ed., *Japanese Ghosts & Demons: Art of the Supernatural* (New York: George Braziller, 1985).

9. Infernal Devices: Automaton Monsters
RESOURCES

Lisa Nocks, *The Robot: The Life Story of a Technology* (Westport, CT: Greenwood Press, 2007).

Wendy Beth Hyman, ed., *The Automaton in English Renaissance Literature* (Burlington, VT: Ashgate Publishing, 2011).

Domenico Laurenza, *Leonardo's Machines: Da Vinci's Inventions Revealed* (Cincinnati: David & Charles, 2006).

Mark Elling Rosheim, *Leonardo's Lost Robots* (Berlin: Springer-Verlag, 2006).

Boston Museum of Science Inventor's Workshop, http://legacy.mos.org/sln /Leonardo/InventorsWorkshop.html.

Patrick Lin, Keith Abney, and George A. Bekey, eds., *Robot Ethics* (Cambridge, MA: MIT Press, 2012).

Daniel Ichbiah, *Robots: from Science Fiction to Technological Revolution* (New York: Harry N. Abrams, 2005).

11. Steampunking You
RESOURCES

Art Donovan, *The Art of Steampunk* (East Petersburg, PA: Fox Chapel, 2011).

Jay Strongman, *Steampunk: The Art of Victorian Futurism* (London: Korero Books, 2011).

12. Resurrecting the Dead and Living Forever

RESOURCES

David Chidester, *Patterns of Transcendence: Religion, Death, and Dying* (Belmont, CA: Wadsworth, 1990).

James H. Hyslop, *Life after Death: Problems on the Future Life and Its Nature* (London: Routledge, 1919).

Sherwood Eddy, *You Will Survive After Death* (New York: Rinehart, 1950).

13. Alchemy and Ouroboros

1. John Read, *Through Alchemy to Chemistry: A Procession of Ideas & Personalities* (London: G. Bell and Sons, 1957), p. 61.

ADDITIONAL RESOURCES

William R. Newman, *Atoms and Alchemy: Chymistry and the Experimental Origins of the Scientific Revolution* (Chicago: University of Chicago Press, 2006).

Grillot de Givry, *Witchcraft, Magic & Alchemy* (Mineola, NY: Dover, 1971).

Sean Martin, *Alchemy and Alchemists* (Great Britain: Harpenden Pocket Essentials, 2001).

15. Real or Not Real?

1. Cheryl Brody, "The Author of CG! Book Club's *City of Ashes* Answers Four Quick Questions Just for You!" www.seventeen.com/entertainment/features/city-of-ashes-cassandra-clare.

2. Donna Freitas, "Q&A with Cassandra Clare," *Publishers Weekly*, March 5, 2009, www.publishersweekly.com/pw/by-topic/authors/interviews/article/12364-q-a-with-cassandra-clare.html.

3. Dani Colvin, "The Power of Love," *Sunday Tasmanian*, Australia, June 3, 2012, p. 24.

19. Mini-Biography of Cassandra Clare

1. Alter, Alexandra, "The New Queen of Fantasy: Cassandra Clare's Breakout," *Wall Street Journal*, June 15, 2012.

2. Dennis McLellan, *Los Angeles Times*, June 17, 2004.

3. www.profilebooks.com/richard-rumelt; www.anderson.ucla.edu/faculty/dick.rumelt/Docs/rumelt_vita.pdf.

4. David A. Kaplan, "A Most Unusual Father-Daughter Professional Pairing," *CNNMoney*, August 29, 2012, features.blogs.fortune.cnn.com/2012/08/29/Cassandra-clare-richard-rumelt.

5. www.cassandraclare.com/faq/what-are-your-personal-goals-what-are-your-goals-for-your-books/.

6. *Authors and Artists for Young Adults*, Volume 86, 2012, p. 50.

7. http://cynthialeitichsmith.blogspot.com/2008/03/author-interview
   -cassandra-clare-on.html.
8. www.cassandraclare.com/faq/did-you-always-want-to-be-a-writer-and
   -this-questions-close-cousin-what-inspired-you-to-be-a-writer/.
9. Lucy Clark, *Sunday Telegraph* (Australia), May 22, 2011.
10. Sarah Moroz, "Saturday in the Park with Cassie," *Publishers Weekly,* August
    25, 2009, www.publishersweekly.com/pw/by-topic/childrens/childrens
    -book-news/article/11805-saturday-in-the-park-with-cassie.html.
11. www.cassandraclare.com/faq/what-is-the-first-thing-you-ever-wrote/.
12. www.voya.com/2012/03/09/wouldn't-you-like-to-know-cassandra-clare/.
13. www.powells.com/kidsqa/clare.html.
14. Moroz, "Sunday in the Park with Cassie."
15. www.cassandraclare.com/faq/where-did-you-get-the-idea-for-the-mortal
    -instruments-books/.
16. Ong, "Monsters, Inc.; Forget Middle Earth."
17. Jewell, "Magical Tales Take on Life of Their Own."
18. www.voya.com/2012/03/09/wouldn't-you-like-to-know-cassandra-clare/.

ADDITIONAL RESOURCE

Robert Colville, "Boldly go where no one has gone before. Imagine Harry Potter in a clinch with James Bond: Welcome to the world of fan fiction," *Daily
Telegraph* (London), January 27, 2007, p. 21.